Lillie,

A Motherless Child

About the Author:

Born and raised in Houston, Texas; Lynn Hobbs moved to East Texas with her family in 1962. She wrote long, thick letters 'back home' many relatives passed around. They enjoyed the descriptions and encouraged her writing, which led to published gospel songs and poetry. Drawn to write short stories and in-depth novels, her passion for writing continues today. Recently retired from the Texas public school system, Lynn writes Christian Fiction: Suspense, Inspiration, and

Romance. Active in church, Karnack Baptist, she serves on several committees.

Lynn is a member of American Christian Fiction Writers, Texas Association of Authors, Pens: Crosswords Christian Writers, East Texas Christian Writers, North East Texas Writers Organization, lifetime member of World Wide Who's Who, and member and past treasurer of East Texas Writers Association.

Lynn Hobbs was awarded 1st place in Religious Fiction 2013, for the first book in The Running Forward Series, "Sin, Secrets, and Salvation" by the Texas Association of Authors. She was awarded 1st Place in Religious Fiction 2014 for the second book in the series "River Town" also by the Texas Association of Authors, and awarded 1st Place in Religious Fiction 2015 for the third book in the series "Hidden Creek" again by the Texas Association of Authors. World Wide Who's

Who awarded her Professional of The Year Representing Authorship 2012-2013.

TheAuthorShow.com named Lynn Hobbs as a winner in their nationwide contest, "Fifty Great Writers You Should Be Reading" in 2013, and as a finalist in 2012. Lynn Hobbs was a winner of 2011 NaNoWriMo, (National Novel Writers Month) where a 50,000 word novel must be written in 30 days at NaNoWriMo.org's website during November for that year. She placed 1st in short story competition with "The Shoe Fit The Wrong

Sister" published in April, 2012 edition of ETWA "The Roughdraft" and 2nd place for "The Song That Changed Everything" published in May 2012 edition of ETWA "The Roughdraft." Her short story "Escape" was published in the June 2012 edition of "Angies Diary" an online e-magazine.

Author of the Running Forward Series; a powerful faith and family saga consists of three books; Sin, Secrets, and Salvation, River Town, and Hidden Creek. Her goal in writing this series is to give readers a clear understanding of a Christian viewpoint by the actions of her main character. All books are available on Tx.Authors.com, Amazon.com, Kindle, Barnes and Noble, and Nook. Her current work in progress is a new Christian Fiction series.

Lynn Hobbs enjoys living on the banks of Big Cypress Bayou at Caddo Lake in Northeast Texas, and is available for book signings, speaking engagements; Christian Retreats, Lions Club, etc. Married; two sons, three grandchildren, two great grandchildren, and two dogs round out the family.

http://www.LynnHobbsAuthor.com

Other works by Lynn Hobbs:

Running Forward Series

    Sin, Secrets, and Salvation

    River Town

    Hidden Creek

Lillie,

A Motherless Child

By Award Winning Author:

Lynn Hobbs

Proof Productions

Karnack, Texas

Lillie, A Motherless Child
Copyright©2015 by Lynn Hobbs

Cover art by Jeff Brannon
Proof Productions

All rights reserved. No part of this book may be reproduced or transmitted in any form or by any electronic or mechanical means, including but not limited to: photocopying; recording or by any information storage and retrieval system, without the express written permission by the author, except where permitted by law.

PRINTED IN THE UNITED STATES OF AMERICA

ISBN-13:978-0692509944 (Proof Productions)

ISBN-10:0692509941

This is the true, inspiring story of the life of

my mother,

Lillie Clark.

I hope you, as a reader enjoy the book. I chose to write it in first person and remained true to Mother's voice.

I dedicate this book to her.

She taught me more about life… by living hers…

and without realizing it at the time… showed me what really matters most.

Ernst Robert Fritsche (birth: 1883, death: 1970) was born in Lee County, Texas. He married Martha Alfreda Bertha Mitschke (birth: 1890, death: 1935); and together, they had 16 children.

This is the true story of their daughter,

Lillie.

Table of Contents

Part I
Chapter 1 …..................... pg. 2
Chapter 2 …..................... pg. 23
Chapter 3 …..................... pg. 35
Chapter 4 …..................... pg. 68
Chapter 5 …..................... pg. 95
Chapter 6 …..................... pg. 116

Part II
Chapter 7 …..................... pg. 136
Chapter 8 …..................... pg. 145
Chapter 9 …..................... pg. 159
Chapter 10 …..................... pg. 173
Chapter 11 …..................... pg. 179
Chapter 12 …..................... pg. 185
Chapter 13 …..................... pg. 217
Chapter 14 …..................... pg. 225
Chapter 15 …..................... pg. 244
Chapter 16 …..................... pg. 258
Chapter 17 …..................... pg. 267
Chapter 18 …..................... pg. 278
Chapter 19 …..................... pg. 314

Chapter 20 …....................... pg. 334
Chapter 21 …....................... pg. 346

Part III
Chapter 22 …....................... pg. 386
Family Photos …................. pg. 417
Lil's Recipes ….................... pg. 424

PART I

Chapter One

"Mama, Mama," I screamed a projected level only a seven year old can master. Overcome by fright, my voice suddenly broke. I jumped up and down in agony. A shrill, high-pitch yell finally sailed out, "Raymond fell in the pond. He's drowning."

"Well, reach in there and pull him out." She called frantically from somewhere inside the house. The windows were wide open. Curtains billowed about in the afternoon breeze.

My four year old sister, Bernice, glanced toward me and emitted a low, mournful wail that escalated to ear-piercing cries. My heart raced. Leaning forward, I could barely see the mass of curls on top of Raymond's head. At two years old, the murky water was sucking him under. Snatching his hair, I yanked the tiny body from the pond, and shoved him onto the grass. He coughed and sputtered.

"Tee, what you make me done?" His anger spat at me.

"See, you got too close. Get back now. Come on." He struggled while trying to raise himself from the grass. I helped him up as Bernice approached.

"Bubba," she said half-aloud, her chin trembling.

"Is Raymond alright?" Mama hollered.

I turned and caught a quick glimpse of him. He was sopping wet and silent. He didn't look hurt. "I got him out, he's okay."

"Bring him and Bernice with you and stay on the porch." Her voice drifted to the back of the house.

Reaching for a hand from each of them, I took my little brother and sister with me. The pond was about twenty-five feet away from the left side of our home.

We walked to the front lawn, past the water well with a hand pump, and slowly made our way to the porch. The wooden house was large and painted white, and Mama had a kitchen garden behind it. We climbed the steps to the front porch and sank into the empty rocking chairs where our parents sat in the evening.

No one came to check on us. I knew Mama was cooking or cleaning.

My name is Lillie, but Daddy calls me Lilla-Mae.

Raymond, Bernice, and I were the youngest of sixteen siblings. Our German family struggled as did countless others during the Great Depression years. First born was Matilda (Tilda), then Edwin (Ed), Olga, Otto,

Ernst, Hattie (Jane), Amanda (May), Marie, Elsie, Rudolph (Bill), Rubin, Lorraine, Lillie, Fredrick (Freddie, died of phenomena at two months old), Bernice, and Raymond. Born in 1928, I was the oldest of the last three siblings and watched after the other two. Our older brothers and sisters were either in school, helping Daddy work in the field, doing daily household chores with Mama, or married and had moved away. Unknown to us children, the depression was in progress. This was our way of life, we were a happy family, and we were loved. If Mama had to stop and run after so many children all day, she would never get anything done. It was natural for us to look after each other.

"Let's play nails." Bernice pleaded after we rocked and sang and finally became bored.

"I guess so. We can stay by the porch." I focused on Raymond and raised my voice. "You stay away from the pond." I scolded. His little face turned slowly towards the ground, and his eyes were almost closed. I watched as the small shoulders on his thin frame shook up and down. He whimpered under his breath, and I realized I had been too hard on him. I knew why he loved the pond. Mama had all of us children stand in line each afternoon, passing a bucket of water from the pond to her kitchen garden. She would stand in front watering the vegetables. Raymond thought watering was fun. That was why he wanted to go near the pond. He wanted all of us to get in a line and pass the sloshing bucket across the lawn to each other. Someone always spilled water on his bare feet, and he'd laugh with excitement. I stopped and hugged him.

"I'm sorry I yelled. " I stammered. Water was still dripping down his face. I shoved wet hair back from his forehead.

"Okay, sister." He patted my arm, his feelings had improved, and I was grateful.

"Raymond, wait here while we get the nails." He flashed a wide lopsided smile, and we were once again buddies.

Retrieving the nails was not an easy task. Crawling under the porch, Bernice and I wiggled across the dirt. A strong, musty smell of damp earth hung in the air and assaulted our nostrils. Totally drenched, Raymond squatted in the sunshine, and extended one open hand under the house. He sifted dirt through his fingers and waited for us to transfer the 'toys' to him. Most of the nails were rusty, all were different lengths. These were our 'people'.

Retrieving them from the front of a brick, we scooted back to Raymond, and placed them in his little hand. He deposited them on the ground, and returned his out-stretched arm toward us again.

"More, bring some more."

"Here come the rooms. Be careful with the glass." I called out to him, and maneuvered back to the brick. Various shapes of an assortment of colored glass lay in a pile. Lifting them cautiously, I dumped all of the pieces into Raymond's hand. Bernice scrambled out from under the house, and I bumped the top of my head as I exited.

Our older sister, Marie, had taught us how to play nails. We would draw a house in the dirt with a stick. A piece of colored glass was placed inside each drawn square to make a 'room'. The nails were the family for our houses. Long nails were the parents, smaller nails were the children. We would name them, and walk our people to each other's houses and talk for them as they would visit each other. We'd play for hours. Our imaginations were based on observing our own families routines, and the conversations we copied were overheard from them. We couldn't afford real toys, and enjoyed pretending.

Bernice and I sprawled on the ground and drew our houses in the dirt. We set up our play area, while Raymond ran to our two older brothers 'cars'. They were Rubin and Rudolph's make believe cars. The two older brothers were in school that day. Raymond eased into the deep, oblong hole each brother had dug in the ground, and sat down, placing his legs inside, also. An old piece of board was always kept inside each car. Our little brother held the car's board up with both hands. This was the 'steering wheel', and he took turns 'driving' each car for the remainder of the afternoon, while Bernice and I played nails.

The drowning episode was quickly forgotten as our laughter filled the air.

Making no attempt to stop playing, we glanced at the commotion from the road as our two older brothers walked home from school. We lived in the countryside of Fairbanks, Texas with few neighbors and had our own farm. Our brothers drifting voices became more distinguishable on their approach to our front lawn.

"Lillie, a jack rabbit chased us all the way home." Rudolph said, frowning at the three younger siblings. Rubin's mouth fell open, and he turned to stare at Rudolph in amazement.

"You are joking, silly Rudolph. Rubin would catch that rabbit and make a pet out of it. Isn't that right, Rubin?"

"I sure would, Lillie. We could all play with him." He grinned and followed Rudolph up the steps to the porch.

"Girl, you caught me joking, again." Rudolph laughed and both boys entered the house.

Later that evening, Mama called us in to eat dinner.

Robert and Martha Fritsche were our parents. Daddy always said the blessing before we ate. I can remember the long, wooden multi-planked table where we all gathered to eat. Mama and Daddy sat at each end and long benches held a mixture of my brothers and sisters on either side. Rubin was 10 years old and Rudolph was 12. They would slide huge bowls of food down the length of the table to reach other family members. Everyone talked at the same time, and it was always cheerful. Dinner went by fast.

This particular evening, Daddy had picked a watermelon from the garden for our enjoyment after dinner. Busy cutting it open, he laughed. "Hard to believe nothing has ever slid off this table and made a mess on the floor."

Rudolph stood and reached for a slice. "That's because we practice so much."

Everyone was ready with outstretched hands as Rubin and Rudolph slid one slice after another down the long table.

I ate a few bites and accidentally swallowed a watermelon seed. I gulped, and Rudolph noticed.

"Oh, your belly is going to get as big as Mama's." He announced.

I knew Mama was big and pregnant nearly every year and Rudolph's warning shocked me. I looked at him wide-eyed and fear engulfed me. I burst out crying. My parents and siblings spoke in unison claiming that wouldn't really happen. I trusted them, and finished my slice of melon.

After eating, our older brothers and sisters cleared the table and washed the dishes. Bernice and I would run out to the porch and try to beat each other to the laps of our parents as they rocked in their rocking chairs. Bernice always crawled into Daddy's lap, and I scrambled to Mama. They held us each evening, and it was such a comforting time.

When Mama tucked me into bed that night, she noticed my dirty feet.

"Lillie, go clean your feet. You can't sleep in bed like that; you'll get those sheets dirty."

"Mama, I'm tired. I promise I'll hang my feet out."

She laughed. "Okay, then, but you better hang them off the bed all night."

"I will." I solemnly told her, and I did.

I had no way of knowing then how much I'd treasure our time together. My mother would pass away within forty-eight hours.

Chapter Two

Morning was unusually quiet. Everyone realized Mother wasn't feeling well. Not her busy, happy self; she sat in a chair in the living room, and Daddy was right by her side.

Always a team, they did everything together. Cooking, gardening, canning; it didn't matter what the task involved. They laughed and shared the work each day.

I don't know whose idea it was to have their game, but they decided to see which one of them could get the fattest. They didn't realize the health risk in those years, so it was fun for the two of them. Mother developed acid indigestion as a result and had to have medication almost daily for it. The fat game quickly stopped.

Daddy got up from his chair and brought her the acid indigestion medicine. It seemed to relieve her. She spent the remainder of the day with Daddy helping her and kidding her about silly things I could hardly hear. Their laughter filled the house, and it was infectious. Everything was back to normal as everyone went to complete their chores. The older children went to school. I, of course, took Raymond and Bernice outside to play.

Her illness returned before dusk fell late that evening.

The sky was alive displaying vivid colors of the sunset when Mama called all of the children to her bedroom. She had us stand around her bed. Daddy wasn't there; I guess he was doing something outside with the animals.

"I want to teach you a Christian song, tonight. I want you to remember it and sing it to me again, sometime." She smiled as she lay in the bed. "It's called, "Revive Us Again."

She taught us the song. We sang it to her, and then we sang it with her. She was overjoyed. We went to bed content, still singing the new song.

The dawn of a new day brought no change to Mother's condition. Our routine continued. Rudolph and Rubin walked to school. Daddy cooked bread soup for Mama. It is an old German recipe he had from his parents that would sooth a stomach ache: one slice of bread torn into pieces, dotted with butter, sprinkled with pepper, and one half cup of hot water poured over the concoction. Mix well. Eat small bites, slowly. It had always worked before. She ate it. Feeling better, she talked, and then rested for a few hours. She awoke with a worsened condition and called out in a weak, quivering voice for Daddy to bring her medicine. He rushed with it, but she was gone before he got to her.

I was outside when she died. I didn't really know what death meant.

~~##~~

Rudolph and Rubin walked home from school on the familiar dusty road. A car drove up from behind them. It passed and suddenly slowed. The word 'Coroner' was printed across the side door.

A man rolled the window down and yelled, "Say, do you boys know where the Fritsche house is?" He squinted against the sun.

"Yes, sir, that is our house."

"Well, get in the car, and show it to us."

Frowning, they climbed into the vehicle obeying adult orders as they were taught.

Rubin whispered, "Rudolph, what does Coroner mean?"

"I don't know."

A few miles later, Rudolph leaned forward from the back seat.

"That's it. That's our home."

The driver veered the car onto the driveway and turned the engine off.

"Boys, you need to go inside. I'm sorry you will have bad news. Tell your daddy we are here."

Rudolph and Rubin gave the men quizzical glances and hurried inside their home. Daddy met them at the front door and embraced them in his arms. As he spoke, the boys cried out in anguish. Daddy cried, and we joined in crying with everyone else. It was a scary moment. My two brothers ran outside, and paced the yard, both wringing their hands and sobbing.

The men from the Coroner's office approached Daddy and entered the house. He took them to his and Mamma's bedroom and shut the door. My older siblings had gathered in the living room weeping and holding onto each other.

The wake was held at my married, older, brother Ed's house. We lived in the country and funeral homes were in the larger cities. Mama was in a casket in Ed's living room. I would skip into the room and play with my younger siblings. We had no idea what it meant for our mother to have passed away. Everyone sang the song she had taught us, 'Revive Us Again,' and also 'Rock of Ages.'

~~##~~

Now, at age eighty-seven, I still get tearful when I sing those two songs in church.

Through the years, the sweet sound of youthful siblings and myself singing with Mother still lingers on my mind. 'Hallelujah, thine the glory, Hallelujah, amen. Hallelujah thine the glory, Revive us again. Revive us again, philly chart with thy love, for Jesus, etc." It was after I turned twelve years old that I discovered 'philly chart' was actually 'fill each heart.' I had already begun experiencing hearing loss at that early stage in my life.

I thought Mama was sleeping in the casket. She was forty-five years old. Many attended the service. Daddy and Mama's parents, grandparents, aunts, uncles, cousins, siblings, and friends followed the procession as we drove to the cemetery. We younger three fidgeted as the preacher talked, and the group mourned.

In 1935, the year she died, they didn't wait until the grieving family left the cemetery. They buried the casket in front of everyone. I remember the moment they lowered Mama's casket into the ground. Bernice and I were okay until that happened.

"No, don't put Mama in that hole." We both repeated our plea and screamed until someone took us away.

Chapter Three

Daddy asked my older sister, Marie, who had an apartment and wasn't married, to come home to our farm in the country and take care of us. Besides myself, young Bernice and Raymond; our teenage sisters, Lorraine and Elsie still lived at home as did our brothers, Rudolph and Rubin. Marie left her job and returned.

It was a busy, new job for her. Daddy had horses, mules, cows, pigs, chickens, plus a huge garden and was out working most of the day. My married, older brothers lived miles away but often came on week-ends to help Daddy. We had no running water, and no electricity. We used kerosene oil lamps, an outhouse for a toilet, and had a water pump.

I loved the water pump. It was new, and the latest model. To obtain water, you had to pump and pump the long handle fast to first prime it before you could get water. We took turns taking Daddy water to drink when he was working in the garden. This was our world that Marie hadn't been a part of in years.

Daddy would plow the garden using his old mule. We also took turns walking along beside the mule, and when she stopped, we had to swish her with a long switch we'd been given. Once when it was my turn, I stumbled and fell. The old mule stepped on my chest, and thankfully, it really didn't hurt that bad.

A favorite place to play for Bernice and I was under the front porch. Our house was about three feet off the ground on blocks, and we had plenty of room. One day we discovered some small white animals and let them crawl on our hands. They were tiny and cute. After several days of returning and finding them still under our porch, we decided to bring them inside. They kept running off so we put them in a paper bag. When Daddy came home from work, we could hardly contain our excitement.

"Daddy, look at the animals we found." I grinned, opened the bag, and picked one up.

"Oh, no. Let me have them."

He took them out the back door and returned in a few minutes without the paper bag or the animals.

"Girls, don't ever play with any of them again, and don't ever bring them back in the house. These are baby mice. They will each grow up to be an awful big mouse that will chase you."

It scared us terribly, and we never touched one again. In fact, we even quit playing under the house.

Bernice turned her attention to cooking. She was too young to cook, but often wanted to make biscuits. She begged Daddy until he finally gave in. I watched. When she took them from the oven and covered them with a towel, her face beamed with pride. The biscuits were part of the evening meal. Rudolph grabbed the first one.

"It's hard as a rock," he exclaimed. "I can't eat this thing."

Rubin took one, pounded it on top of the table, and laughed.

Bernice was in tears as she watched her brothers.

"That's enough, boys. Your sister was kind enough to make the biscuits, and you will be kind enough to eat them. No one leaves this table until they apologize to Bernice and eat their biscuits." They apologized and Bernice was satisfied she could cook. No one mentioned the biscuits again, and we were all happy when Bernice tired of cooking. Her new decision to try sweeping and cleaning was whole-heartily encouraged by everyone.

Bernice and I would spread a quilt out in the yard on cloudy days. We enjoyed lying on our backs, gazing at the clouds, and using our imagination.

"Sister, that cloud looks like a fluffy rabbit." Bernice would point towards the sky.

"It does. Over here, I see a house, and there is a doll…" I flung my arm upward to show her.

"I see a cross, look at that."

She and I could visualize for hours thoroughly happy.

Rudolph and Rubin enjoyed helping Daddy, going to school and church, and were also the comics of our family. In order to become a member of our Missouri Synod Lutheran church, you had to take confirmation classes of Bible instruction when you reached the age of twelve. One night, Rudolph was returning home after confirmation class. He'd previously told all of us about the Holy Ghost.

Rubin was waiting outside in the dark covered in a white sheet. Rudolph approached the front steps and younger Rubin jumped out from the side of the house moaning and groaning deeply, waving his arms about under the sheet. Terrified, Rudolph ran inside the house screaming, "A ghost is after me, Daddy, a ghost is after me." Daddy found Rubin outside still moaning, and promptly pulled the sheet off of him. After a stern discussion, Rubin never played ghost again.

Mischievous ways continued, though. Weeks later, Rudolph and Rubin caught several huge frogs at the pond, and placed them in a large canning jar. Air holes were made in the lid with a pocket knife to keep the frogs alive. Sitting side by side on the porch one day with the jar of frogs croaking loudly between them, younger brother Raymond walked towards them. Raymond couldn't pronounce Rudolph and for some reason called him "Whody."

"Raymond, look at our talking frogs. They can talk."

Raymond stopped and listened as the frogs croaked intently. "Whody, you know what those frogs are saying?"

Rudolph kept a straight face. "What?"

"They are saying, 'Oh man, let us out of here.' I have to go play." Raymond yelled with a frightened glance at the frogs and ran off.

Rudolph and Rubin laughed at their little brother and teased him often about the talking frogs.

I think they got the teasing from our daddy's father. He was a jolly person who loved children and laughed often. Our grandfather even built us kids a long see-saw. We loved to play on it. I can remember taking turns and sailing high into the air with my legs extended. We were a lively bunch of kids.

I presume that Marie must have been overwhelmed at caring for our lively group.

One afternoon, Bernice and Raymond fell in a mud puddle, and she had to give them a bath. It was impossible for her to watch me at the same time. I went to the chicken yard to see the baby chicks. When they stuck their little heads through the holes in the wire fence, I would grab their necks and try to pull them out. Thus I killed eighty-five baby chicks and didn't know they died because I broke their necks. Poor baby chicks. Poor Marie. What an awful financial loss to the family income. Daddy lost his temper and really scolded Marie for not having Lorraine or Elsie watch me while she was busy.

He never got onto me. He did patiently explain that I was not to do that again. I never got a spanking in my life.

We loved our Daddy, dearly. We'd ask him to play his harmonica, and he would play it often for us. Lorraine had given me a treasured bottle of nail polish that still had a little bit left in the bottle. Daddy did let Bernice and I polish his toe-nails, but only the one large toe on each foot. He'd let us practice combing his hair in different styles after the nail polishing. He spent a lot of time with all of us. He was a sweet, caring man.

I think Daddy sensed how much I still missed Mother. He would silently pat me on my back when I mentioned her. I could no longer remember what she looked like, and it bothered me. I never did overcome the emptiness of not having her in my life, and often reflected how it would be if other women I'd meet would end up being my mother. Finally, I discussed it with Daddy, and we prayed about it.

The following day, he asked me and Bernice if we'd like to have a vacation and visit his sister, Rosie, and her family for two weeks. We liked them and couldn't wait for the trip. They lived in Giddings, Texas; had a farm, children our ages, and they had cows.

We had a wonderful two weeks. Every evening the cows would come home for the night to eat. One cow was stubborn and sometimes wouldn't follow the others back from the pasture. We were told to go find her. She'd be hiding behind trees, or standing in a shallow creek-bed. It was difficult getting her to leave the hiding places. She simply didn't want to come home.

We also visited our mother's brother, our Uncle David. He had a cotton gin and also lived in Giddings, Texas near our father's sister, Aunt Rosie's, home. Uncle David and his wife had several children, and a twenty foot long see-saw. It was the most thrilling see-saw, and we'd yell with excitement as we went high up in the air. I'll never forget that one. I'd hold onto each side of the board I sat on, so tight, my hands would tremble. Our family certainly provided for their kids to enjoy play time!

Once while I was at Aunt Rosie's, I took off exploring by myself. I climbed over a fence and wandered around a bit, when a huge bull suddenly appeared and started charging me. I certainly wasn't expecting a thousand pound bull to be chasing me, much less at full speed. I could hear my heart pounding in my ears while I ran as fast as I could go. The sight and sound of the bull completely terrified me. He snorted loudly through his nostrils. When the impact of his hoofs hit the ground, carrying a tremendous amount of weight, it seemed to shake the ground like thunder. He was still in hot pursuit as I climbed over the fence and kept running. I had never been so scared before.

Our father's brother, Walter Fritsche, also lived in Giddings, and had a grocery store out in the country. Aunt Rosie took us to visit Uncle Walter before we returned home. He let us have handfuls of candy from the barrels inside. We loved our vacation, and thanked our relatives for our time together. Returning home, we told everyone about our experiences, especially Marie.

She was fun, and a good cook. I was glad my older sister was still at our home. She had been dating Forrest Goodwin before she came to take care of us. He drove out to the farm to continue seeing her, until he happened to meet Elsie. One year younger than her sister Marie, Elsie was more petite, and mischievous. Daddy wouldn't let anyone visit his daughters alone until the girls were at least seventeen, and he was nearby. Elsie was sixteen, but that didn't stop Forrest. He arranged to meet Elsie in the corn field late one evening. They quickly eloped and got married. Marie was heartbroken, and Daddy was angry. Time passed and tensions eased as Forrest and Elsie proved to everyone how they were meant for each other. Marie even wished them well. Daddy remained distant to Forrest and didn't trust him.

Marie met Otto Proske at church a month later. They fell in love and couldn't stand to be apart from each other. He came often to visit her and kept her behind in her chores. Bernice, Raymond, and I were watched less and less as Otto became more infatuated with Marie. One such day Otto and Marie sat on the porch talking, and I wandered off to the back yard. Daddy had several large, stone crocks he used to make pickles and sauerkraut. An empty one was outside. I sat on it. My little rear-end sunk down inside. I couldn't get out.

"Marie!" I wailed.

She and Otto came running. They attempted to get me released, but it was useless.

"Daddy, come help." She hollered.

He hurried and tried to pull me out. It didn't work. I kept crying, frightened that I'd be stuck forever.

"Rudolph, bring me a hammer." Daddy yelled, and Rudolph wasted no time.

"Hit the crock while I hold her." He instructed while tightening his grip around my waist and pushing my legs into the air.

Rudolph swung the hammer into the side of the crock. It broke, and I was free. This was during the depression, and it was a huge loss to Daddy. I didn't get in trouble, though. He stood me onto the ground and sighed.

Lorraine had heard the yelling and witnessed my rescue. I had not noticed her during my ordeal. Embarrassed, I felt Daddy pat me on my back. Everyone was relieved I was unhurt, and we all ambled back to the house.

"Daddy, I saw some men on our property yesterday morning on our way to school." Rudolph mentioned.

"Where? What were they doing?"

"I meant to say something and forgot about it. They were way out in the back pasture, walking around carrying some tools.

They left when they saw me…took off in a hurry."

Daddy stopped and rubbed his hand across his chin. "Humpf. Let me know if they come back."

"I will."

"Hey, I have some good news." Lorraine's face beamed with excitement. "I entered a contest, and I think I might win."

"What kind of contest?" Daddy sighed.

"It's a contest to name the Shirley Temple doll. I chose the name 'Dimples.' I think it's perfect, don't you?"

"Yes. You did well, Lorraine. I hope you win."

We went inside and made dinner preparations. After we ate, Daddy sat quietly on the porch. He starred at the rusty old mailbox standing near the road, and finally stood and stretched. He meandered to the mailbox and retrieved a few envelopes. Lost in thought, he thumbed through them, and jerked his head close to one of them. He ripped it open and seemed to be mesmerized.

"What is it, Daddy?" I tugged at his pants leg.

"Oh, I have to drive into town tomorrow."

"Can I go?"

"No, Lilla-Mae. I have to go to the bank."

He grew quiet, and our family later turned in for the night. Daddy had already left when I awoke. I had breakfast and waited for him by the road. Before Marie told us lunch was ready, Daddy returned.

"Everyone come into the kitchen." His voice was shaky.

We surrounded him and heard the stomping of Rubin's boots as he rushed into the room. Daddy carefully looked at us and smiled. Daddy was the sweetest man I knew and kind to everyone. I had only seen him angry twice in my life; once at Marie, and once at Forrest and Elsie.

"I don't like to tell you my business, but I have no choice. The bank is going to foreclose on us in thirty days. They want all of the mortgage money at one time, not the monthly payment plan we agreed to. I am not behind on my payment, but that doesn't matter. I don't have the money to pay the entire loan off."

He glanced at us and sighed. "You won't understand any of this, but we have to move. I have decided we will move to Houston."

Excitement filled the air as each young sibling whooped and hollered. Not understanding Daddy's predicament, I thought it was time to celebrate. Judging from their actions, at least Bernice and Raymond must have felt the same way I did.

Within two weeks, Lorraine won the Shirley Temple doll contest. She received eight hundred dollars, and promptly gave it to Daddy. Although it was not enough to pay off the loan, it was enough to build a house along with the building materials grandfather donated. Daddy left Marie in charge of us and met his father in Houston.

My married older sister, Olga, had assured Daddy she would watch after Bernice, Raymond, and me when we moved. He bought two lots in Houston a few houses down from her house. His father, who also lived in Houston, along with other family members, built the house we would live in for many years. It was a two bedroom home with a large front porch. One double bed was in one bedroom for Bernice and I to share, and a set of bunk beds was in the other bedroom for Daddy and Raymond. A new see-saw was also built. When the building of the house was completed, we left the farm in Fairbanks, Texas, and Marie married Otto Proske.

After we moved to Houston, oil was discovered on our old property that was now owned by the bankers. The massive oil derrick went up on the back pasture exactly where my brothers saw the strange men walking around carrying tools.

Many farmers lost their land to unscrupulous bankers during the depression in the early 1930's, especially if thick, black oil was discovered on the property.

Chapter Four

Our home was on Pickfair Street, two blocks from Kashmere Gardens Elementary school, and four blocks from Our Savior Lutheran church. It was in 1934 that I started first grade at the public school. The church became a large part of my life. City living had its perks. It was a quiet neighborhood, comfortable and friendly. Lorraine moved in with the Miller family. She loved living with them. Rubin and Rudolph moved in with our older sister, Elsie, and her husband, Forrest Goodwin. The arrangement worked well.

Olga and Herman Grimm had married years earlier and lived in the German settlement of Giddings, Texas. Many of our relatives still lived there. They later had their first child; a daughter named Alene, and moved to Houston. Alene was my age and although I was actually her aunt, I would become her best friend for over eighty years.

Alene and I started first grade at the same time. We walked to school together.

"Lillie, I want you to watch out for Alene. She has fainting spells quite often."

"I will, Olga." I solemnly told her; after all I was Alene's aunt.

The first day of school, the teacher handed each one of us a form to take to our mothers.

"No one but your mother is to sign this, no one!" She instructed. The bell rang for recess, and we all ran outside. Once I was outside, I started crying.

"What is wrong?" A little girl shyly asked.

"I don't have a Mother," I cried.

She started crying with me. Other children approached us.

"What happened?" They asked.

The little girl pointed at me, and her voice shook as she spoke. "She doesn't have a Mother."

Eventually, seven little girls stood next to me by a tree, and we were crying together. The bell rang, and the teacher came outside.

"Why are you girls crying?" She stood with her hands on her hips.

All of the classmates spoke at once. "She doesn't have a Mother." They sobbed even louder as they glanced at me and back at each other.

I'm sure the teacher was more careful in the future with the wording of her instructions.

She had us enter the classroom that evening, and we cried randomly for hours.

A few days later, during recess, Alene fainted while standing next to me. I gasped and ran away as fast as I could. I was so scared. The teacher helped her, and she was finally okay.

Daddy did his best to take care of us and work. He was fortunate in securing a job at the shipyards. My hearing problems worsened. I began having boils in both of my ears. Daddy would have to take me to an ear specialist, and the doctor would lance the boils. It was too painful for anyone, much less a first grade child. Other than my ears, none of us were ever sick, not even with a head cold.

We had excellent attendance at school, and Daddy soon had us in Sunday school at our church. Daddy had to work week-ends. He woke us up on Sunday morning, and told us to get dressed for Sunday school. He would go on to work. Each Sunday morning, my brother-in-law, Herman Grimm, rang the church bell at eight o'clock. You could hear it ringing for miles.

If we didn't show up for Sunday school, Mr. Koch, (pronounced Cook) a teacher at the Lutheran church, would come to our house, walk in, wake us up and make us come to Sunday school. He was a young man, never married. I didn't like him. When I was in the third grade, our church started a school there for grades one through seven. Daddy transferred us from the public school to the private Lutheran school. Mr. Koch took it upon himself to look after Bernice, Raymond, and myself. He would check on us each morning at school. Raymond had a bad habit of keeping his fingers by his nose. Mr. Koch often made Raymond leave the classroom to go wash his hands. He never found anything wrong with Bernice or me.

Between eight and nine years old, I found myself raising Bernice and Raymond while Daddy worked. I did okay until one day when I was washing dishes, and Bernice was drying them with a dish towel; she became a little sassy and made me mad. I took the wet, soapy dishcloth and mopped her face with it. She behaved after that.

One morning, I was about to leave the house and walk to the store when Bernice stopped me.

"I want to go with you." She pleaded.

I looked at her long blonde hair, a tangled mess. It could be so beautiful when brushed. "You have to comb your hair."

"I don't want to."

"Okay, I'll tell everyone we meet that you are not my sister."

She grinned, and followed me out the door. Raymond remained at home. He usually went with us, but he preferred playing outside with his red wagon. As we advanced down the street, we came across a man on the opposite side.

I glanced at him. "See that girl?" I motioned behind me at Bernice.

"Yes."

"That is not my little sister."

He seemed puzzled and walked on.

She told me years later how that hurt her and to this day (I'm 87 years old) I feel bad about it.

We returned from the store and darted into the kitchen. Totally on our own, we did everything together. Bernice and I would cook something to eat each day after school. Sometimes we'd fry eggs for an egg sandwich, or fry a slice of ham. We loved to fry food. Often, we had kitchen fires. Today was no different.

"Help me with these potatoes, sister." I motioned to Bernice. She climbed on her stool near the sink and grabbed the potato peeler. I placed a bowl of water at one end of the long sink. Bernice knew to rinse each potato when she finished and throw it into another bowl at the opposite end of the same sink. That is where I cut them into slices and cut again to form the shape of French fries. We loved French fries with ketchup.

The cast iron skillet stayed on top of the stove. I dug shortening out of a can with a long handled spoon and plopped it into the skillet. Half way through frying, fire suddenly shot up into the air. I guess we had the flame too high on the stove. We raced out of the kitchen and nearly fell down hurrying next door to Mrs. Spragen.

"Fire, fire, fire." We hollered as we bolted to where she lived. Her house was about fourteen feet from our house. She rushed over and put out the fire on the stove. This happened at least once a week. Poor Mrs. Spragen, she never complained.

It was a miracle the fires from our cooking didn't burn down the house. We were simply taking care of ourselves and were happy. After school homework in the afternoon, we'd stay busy with chores. Anyone passing by our house could hear us happily singing out loud and making up the words as we sang.

Bernice and I always loved to sing. When the song, "You Are My Sunshine" was released, we sang it often. We missed our mother immensely, and decided to change the words in the song to have more meaning about us and Mother. While Daddy was at work, we rewrote the song after school. Here is our version:

"You are my sunshine, my only sunshine. You make me happy, when skies are gray. You'll never know, Mom, how much we miss you; and we're sorry you passed away.

"The other night, Mom, as I lay sleeping, I dreamed that you were at my side. But when I woke, Mom, I was mistaken, and I hung my head and cried.

"You are my sunshine, etc."

We were proud of our song. Remember we were very young. When Daddy came home and later was in bed for the night, we went into his bedroom.

"Daddy, we have a song to sing to you."

Clearly drowsy, he managed to sit up in bed and nodded his head.

We sang it to him, and he started crying. His crying confused us and at first we had our feelings hurt. He then grabbed and hugged us hard, and we felt better. After I was older, I realized how our singing that song must have hurt Daddy.

Each morning, after breakfast, Daddy prepared our lunch before he went to work. This morning, I watched as he made tuna fish salad for sandwiches. As he stirred the concoction, I remembered it was the first of April, April fool's day.

"Daddy," I sucked in my breath, "There's a bug in that bowl of tuna fish."

"What?" He frowned and slowly spooned through the mixture for several minutes.

"Well, I don't see a bug." He muttered and retrieved a larger bowl from the cabinet. He cautiously examined each chunk of pickle, onion, and apple in the tuna salad and plopped it into the larger bowl. A quick glance at the wall clock confirmed my dilemma. My joke was taking too long. I squirmed as Daddy, determined to find the bug, continued removing one spoonful of tuna salad at a time into the larger bowl.

I waited for half a second longer and knew I had gone too far. "April fool." I yelled and ran from the kitchen. Daddy threw the spoon down, shoved the bowls into the ice box and hurried outside to his truck. He left for work, and I hoped he wouldn't be late because of me. I never played another April fool's joke on him again.

Raymond still followed us around, but he was now in first grade, getting older, and exploring more. I missed him one afternoon and couldn't find him. We had been home from school for at least two hours. He wasn't anywhere in the house. I rushed outside.

"Raymond! Raymond, you better come here!" I yelled, but got no response.

Bernice ran to the end of the driveway and spotted him.

"There he is." She pointed down the street.

In the middle of the street, nearly two blocks away, was our little brother. He was pulling his red wagon, slowly making his way home.

We waited as he came into our yard. My mouth fell open when I noticed what was in his wagon.

"Dishes? Where did you get these dishes?" I grabbed one and examined it. The pattern had pink, intertwined roses that circled near the edge of the heavy cream colored plate. One large rose was painted in the center.

"I got them for Daddy for Father's Day." Raymond beamed.

"Who gave them to you?"

"Nobody, I found them."

"Where?"

"In that building where they have meetings."

"Raymond, did you go into the community center building?"

"Yes, I did."

"How? Did someone let you in?"

"No. I opened the window and climbed inside."

"That is stealing, Raymond. We don't steal."

"I wanted to get them for Daddy." He insisted.

"I know these are nicer than the dishes we have, but it is wrong to steal. Don't you know Mama is in Heaven and can see everything we do? She wants us to be good."

He looked at me wide-eyed. "I won't ever steal again, I promise."

"Well, I have to tell Olga, anyway. Come on, Bernice; let's walk to Olga's house."

"No," Raymond cried. "Don't get me in trouble."

I marched off with Bernice right at my heels. We could still hear Raymond crying as we walked four houses down the street to our big sister's home. We both banged on the door and finally stopped. No one was there. We returned to our own home.

"Olga wasn't home. Don't you ever do anything like this *again*."

He hung his head. "I won't. I'm sorry, sister."

That was the first and last time he stole anything. He did give Daddy the dishes. I'm sure Daddy thought they came from one of our older sisters or brothers. As kids, we didn't want Raymond getting into trouble with Daddy, and Daddy really needed the dishes. As an adult, I realize that was no excuse, but as a kid, I was trying to be the Mother in charge.

A week later, Daddy came in from work late at night and found Raymond lying on the living room floor close to the gas Dearborn heater. Fall had arrived and nights were chilly. Bernice and I were asleep in our bed.

Raymond was beet red and barely breathing. The room was entirely too hot.

Snatching the child to his chest, he rubbed his son until he awoke, and returned to normal. Assured Raymond wasn't harmed; he carried the little boy to bed, returning to lower the flame on the heater.

I heard Daddy mutter to himself, "I have to find them homes…they can no longer stay here alone…"

I went to sleep wondering about it, but I trusted Daddy and wasn't afraid.

Chapter Five

Daddy continued spending quality time with us when he was home from work. A natural born story teller, he kept us entertained for hours.

Once, he told us he had gone to sleep thinking about our mother. In his dream, she stood near his bed and talked to him. He said they discussed their love for each other, and he suddenly realized how real the dream seemed. He quickly awoke to find his hand in the air as if someone held it. Daddy said the dream never happened again.

Some other stories he shared with us concerned his work. One of the jobs Daddy had was being a deputy for our rural area in Fairbanks, Texas.

On this particular week, the High Sheriff gave the description of a stranger that was in our county. The man's dark hair and beard were unkempt, and he wore an old soiled shirt with baggy pants. His overall sloppy appearance was made more noticeable by his habit of acting suspicious. He would duck his head and not look anyone in the eye. Daddy was warned that the stranger was a hobo that caught rides on the empty rail cars on trains.

Vagrants were not allowed in our county as many had broken into homes and stole whatever they could use while the homeowners were gone to work. Many were looking for this hobo.

Then it happened.

Early one morning before Daddy went to work, he weeded his garden. When he finished, he left the back yard and walked toward our house. He noticed something move across the street behind a spindly bush. Squinting for a better view, Daddy's pace increased until he reached the pavement. At that moment, a slovenly man matching the exact description of the hobo, darted out from behind the bush and fled to the street.

Still clutching the hoe by the long handle, Daddy waved it over his head and yelled, "fella, don't let the sun come down on your back with you still here."

The man looked down at the street with his mouth wide open and ran completely out of sight in just a few minutes.

It was not common to see such a person in our neighborhood. To my knowledge, he was the only one, and everyone assumed by his appearance that he was indeed the hobo.

We enjoyed Daddy's story and thought he was brave. He didn't tell us about any of it until the man ran away, so we weren't frightened.

Another encounter was with a man that was a known crook. Riding horseback, Daddy had chased this man out of the woods. The sound of the horses four hooves thudded into the ground loudly as he galloped after the man nonstop. Panting, the crook reached a wide drainage ditch full of water, and Daddy quickly rode up behind the man. Daddy told us he thought he had the man trapped. Suddenly, the man took a deep breath and starred at the wide ditch then glanced back at Daddy. The horse high stepped and walked sideways for a few moments. Daddy pulled the reins up.

"Whoa, boy." He patted the animal's neck.

The horse whinnied, and Daddy steadied it as he unmounted.

The crook didn't hesitate. He took another deep breath, slightly lowered his shoulders and made a dash straight to the ditch.

He took one mighty leap across and made it safety to the other side.

"All I ever saw was the white bottoms of his feet in the air as he sailed over." Daddy told us. "I sure didn't think anyone could jump that 6 foot wide ditch."

Another story he told us was about a man stealing meat from a neighbor's smokehouse. That man was caught and went to jail. Daddy's stories were always exciting.

He loved us dearly, and we loved him with all our heart. Either with stories, the harmonica, or painting toe-nails, it was always a treasured, fun time for us to be together.

We also prayed together, often. Not only to bless our food at meals, but to give thanks for our blessings and ask for forgiveness of our sins. We developed a habit of whatever came our way, we always prayed about it.

I realize now what a difficult decision Daddy had to make about our care. We three children didn't know it was dangerous for us to be alone while he worked.

Daddy went to our church and asked for their help. We knew everyone there and considered the church members as part of our own family. We worshiped together, ate together, and enjoyed many church activities together.

They found homes for the three of us. Raymond was six years old, a cute little guy with blond hair and blue eyes. The young couple he went to had no children, and were eager to have him live with them. Bernice went to an older couple who were also childless. I had to go to my older married brother, Ed, his wife Iweena, and their five boys. They had a set of twins under two years old, one son three years old and two older boys. I had to sleep with the twins, and the three year old. They wet the bed every night, and I couldn't stand this.

Weeks later, Daddy got a call from the young couple who took Raymond. "Mr. Fritsche? You have to come get your son. He is crying so hard and keeps saying he wants his daddy. He crawled up into the attic and won't come out. We're afraid he is going to get sick, crying that hard."

Daddy left immediately and went after Raymond. He later told us that Raymond held unto him for days. Someone phoned Daddy a few days later and reported that the man was trying to molest Bernice where she was living. Daddy rushed over and brought her home.

That was when I called him, still hurting, and said I didn't want to stay with Ed and Iweena anymore. Moments earlier, she had removed a six foot by three foot wooden table top from the kitchen, and had me hold it on its sides, outside. She wanted to clean it. Iweena poured half of the boiling water from a huge, number three size galvanized wash tub, up onto it. I was standing behind it, holding it up. My entire body was scalded. Daddy came and got me.

We three kids were finally back home and happy.

Daddy hired a housekeeper, and a cook to come each day to our house. The cook, Verna, was an attractive woman. After a while, she convinced Daddy to let her live there, and be both cook and housekeeper. He agreed. Later, they started dating. She then talked him into marrying her, and he did. Not realizing how manipulating she was, Daddy was joyful, and at first, Verna was good to us. As a married woman, and our stepmother, her treatment to us three soon changed. She made us do all the work, and she'd lie on the couch until Daddy came home. Naturally, we no longer liked our stepmother.

Once, she got mad with little Raymond, pulled her hand back and repeatedly hit him hard against his ear. She made it bleed. When Daddy got home from work, we told him what happened. He saw the dried blood in

Raymond's ear, took several deep breaths, and confronted Verna.

"When my wife, Martha, was sickly, before she died, she asked me to look after each of the kids but especially Raymond. He is so small and frail. Verna, I can't let you hurt any of them. I'll pack your things."

Verna widened her angry eyes towards us and marched out of the room. Daddy packed her belongings, no one said another word. He carried her suitcases, escorted her out to his truck, and drove her back to her son's home. Good riddance.

I was once again in charge of Bernice and Raymond. Olga was supposed to watch after us, but didn't. With fifteen brothers and sisters, it resembled two separate families; the older ones had bonded with each other, and we younger brothers and sisters grew up apart from them. Some of our nieces and nephews were older than we were. When the soap opera, "As The World Turns" came on television, my school friends talked about it. I wanted to watch it. Since we didn't have a television, I'd walk down the road to Olga's house. Olga was always a happy woman. I can recall hearing her laughter ring out with merriment, but she was also extremely busy. She wouldn't let me inside her house, though, and I didn't understand why. Olga had me sit outside on the porch and listen to the television through the opened window. I never did tell Daddy. I'm sure he would have pointed out how Olga had three sons, Charles, Larry, and El Roy; two daughters, Alene and Ruby Lee, and a husband who she cooked for three times a day. (He came home from work for lunch.) After she cleaned her living room that housed the television, she had no spare time to clean again if her little sister forgot to wipe dirt off of her shoes. That room was already clean for the day.

~~##~~

We three enjoyed hearing anything about our mother. Daddy often told us stories about how much she loved us. This particular Easter, Daddy told Raymond, Bernice, and I how

Mother dyed eggs for us. We were too young to remember.

"Just before dark, your mother would go out to the pasture, cut long, green grass, and return home with armfuls of it. She made the Easter Bunnies' nest by arranging a huge circle about three feet round, and filled it with grass. Then, after everyone went to bed at night, she colored boiled eggs and placed them outside on the cool grass. Every Easter morning, she'd wake you by sprinkling water on our faces. 'Wake up, the Easter Bunny has been here, hurry. Come and see.' She'd say. She dyed lots of eggs for her grandchildren in Houston and elsewhere."

"I remember her sprinkling the water." I blurted.

"Daddy does our eggs, now." Bernice chimed in.

"But how did the grandchildren get their eggs from her?" I pondered aloud.

"I buy the grass at the store, Bernice, and Lilla-Mae, the grandchildren's parents would come and get the eggs for their children." He winked at me, and I treasured his story of a new memory about Mother.

We four loved being together, and we kids had learned to be safer. At twelve years old, Daddy even let me sing in the choir at church with six other girls. Life was good.

Chapter Six

Mr. Koch continued to teach us. He was a great music director. By the time I turned sixteen years old, our singing church group sounded incredibly beautiful. We also sang at other churches and at funerals, etc. Word of mouth spread the news about our splendid singing.

We began singing once a week on a radio station program, where our pastor would give the sermon, and we would sing. The church school would let us check out early. We'd catch the city bus and ride to the KPRC radio station in Houston, Texas. We continued singing on the radio for years.

Bernice and Lil singing on KPRC Radio in Houston, TX.

Once, when we left the radio station, we went to a restaurant to eat. We ordered spaghetti and meatballs. Our meal arrived without the bread. We waited and waited for the bread, but to no avail. Instead of complaining, we both happily sang, "You Get No Bread With One Meatball," which was a popular song then. Our bread soon arrived. We thoroughly enjoyed ourselves that day.

My Lutheran church school stopped at the seventh grade. I was then tested in public school at John Reagan High School, and was way above average— bypassing the eighth grade.

Mary Ellen, my friend since attending elementary Lutheran school, followed me to public school. We had even attended confirmation classes together, and on our first day to catch the city bus to our new public school; she pulled me aside from the others waiting for the bus.

"Lillie, I know your daddy calls you Lilla-Mae. I think it's time we changed your name to something shorter. I'm changing your name to Lil."

"I like Lil." I smiled at my friend, and Lil I became.

When I told Daddy, he chuckled and tried to say Lil, but Leo came out of his mouth. He continued to call me Lilla-Mae for the rest of his life.

I went straight to the ninth grade and completed it. In the tenth grade, my heritage became an issue. Students suddenly harassed me, because of World War II with the Germans, and my German last name, Fritsche. One afternoon while Daddy was at work, the

Houston police came into our home and confiscated the large, elaborate, German-printed Bible that had been in our family for generations. The police claimed it may contain coded German messages pertaining to the war. Daddy was furious when he came home from work. We never saw our family Bible again. It was too much for me to experience. With classmates calling me names at school, and snickering at me in the hallways; the terrible treatment was something I could no longer endure. I decided to quit school. I checked myself out of school the following day.

Daddy came home late that evening.

"I quit school today."

"Oh no, you go back in the morning."

The subject was closed. I returned and stayed to complete the eleventh grade. Boys eighteen and older had to go to war. Because of this, schools let both boys and girls graduate in the eleventh grade, instead of the twelfth. I was seventeen years old when I graduated and received my diploma. I realize now that Daddy wanted me to have an education for my future life, and knew my tormentors wanted to see me fail.

Daddy was awfully strict with us girls. He wouldn't let us wear red nail polish, and all sorts of things. On my first date, I couldn't believe Daddy said I could even go. When my date and I walked out of my house to the boy's car, there was my brother Rubin sitting in the back seat. I was so embarrassed. Daddy made Rubin go as a chaperone.

World War II began and Rubin and Rudolph were off to a foreign war. We were on rations along with everyone else. Daddy had six sons and five were in the Army at the same time. He worried about them constantly. Once, he didn't hear from my brother Rubin for six months. No letters came. Daddy was sick with worry. Raymond, Bernice, and I pleaded with him to take us to a movie.

"Daddy, it will be a wonderful treat. You need it as much as we do." I urged.

He took us.

During the movie, a newsreel came on showing a video of the soldiers leaving the front lines of a successful battle and walking to a new assignment. There in the group was my brother, Rubin. Our daddy yelled for joy, and that's how we knew he was still alive. We four sat there, crying, and gave thanks to God.

At this same time, I liked a young man who lived down the street from us. He joined the Army, and we corresponded by mail. He came home on leave and on a date, he proposed marriage, giving me a ring. When he took me home, and I got inside my house, I was so happy I told Daddy and showed him my ring.

"Oh, no, no, no." He shook his head. "You go right over there and give the ring back."

I was heartbroken, but I did as Daddy told me. I took the ring back to George Ikenburger. George later married one of my girlfriends.

My sister, Elsie, came and got Bernice and I to live with her for a while. I guess it was too quiet at her house with my brothers Rubin and Rudolph gone from her home and off to war. She would take us to the bus stop every morning for Bernice to go to school and for me to go to my new temporary secretarial job. That had been my goal in life— becoming a secretary. Needless to say, I was thrilled, again.

One morning when Elsie arrived back home, she heard a noise in the house. She leaned over to look out the window and received a hard blow on her head. The police later decided the intruder was a German spy living undetected in the attic. The man then slashed Elsie's throat from ear to ear. Forrest, Elsie's husband, was at work and seldom returned home until the end of the day. Something made him return home that morning, and he found my sister lying in a pool of blood. He phoned for an ambulance, and they rushed Elsie to the hospital. Forrest's mother lived in a small guest house behind him and Elsie's home. His mother came and cleaned up everything at the crime scene. Not one drop of blood could be found later, and Elsie had lost nearly all of the blood from her body. Someone said later that the Mother-in-law may have had something to do with what happened to Elsie. I'm not sure about that, but I know they were not the best of friends. And, I know for a fact it's a miracle my sister Elsie didn't die. Forrest and Elsie were friends with the Houston Police Department. Everyone on the force went to donate blood, and they saved her life. Neighbors later stated they saw lights from the attic during the night, weeks before Elsie's throat was cut. Forrest and Elsie remember hearing sounds after retiring to bed but couldn't tell where the slight noises were coming from.

It remains a mystery. I often wondered if the same officers knew Elsie was related to our Fritsche family with the confiscated German Bible. Probably not.

Bernice and I left. We could no longer be comfortable at Elsie's home.

We returned home to Daddy and continued singing. Our music director entered me, Bernice, and my girlfriends in a music contest. We were in a quartet. There were many participants, and our group won. Later, Mr. Koch formed a group of 45 or more women for a choir, I was included, but not Bernice. It seemed strange for her not to be with me at rehearsals and performances. The new group, "The Lutheran Choir", was spectacular. We traveled by bus to different towns to perform. A Hollywood agent contacted the parents of six of us girls in the group for permission to come and sing there. We were excited. None of our parents would let us go. Daddy shook his head again.

"No," he explained. "Lilla-Mae, you are a smart girl, but crooks are there who can take advantage of you and your girlfriends. It's not a good place to be without a chaperone."

"Well, I do understand." I sighed. "I like to sing, but I can do that here." We smiled at each other in agreement. I remained with The Lutheran Choir for several years until my sister, Lorraine, contacted me. I hadn't seen her in quite a while.

Lorraine had remained with the Miller family for many years, and had first met her future husband, D.A. when they attended the fifth grade together at Trinity Lutheran Day School. They also went to the same church, and he would sit with her, but they had nothing to do with each other until high school. Lorraine went to John Reagan High School, and in 1943 they married. D.A. was now a Lutheran pastor, and they invited me to live with them. I gladly did.

Lil Fritsche in a field of Texas Bluebonnets

PART II

Chapter Seven

"D.A. is treating us to lunch. Come on, Lil, let's hurry."

The restaurant was directly across the street. We hurried out of the house, and waited as D. A. locked the door. Then we waited again for the light to change and crossed the street. Traffic was steadily increasing as the noon hour arrived. Horns honked at other vehicles slow to leave the red light. Engines roared as cars accelerated past the intersection.

The noise level quickly caught your attention as activity increased.

The restaurant loomed ahead. It was rare to eat out, and a treat for all three.

"We got here before the rush." Lorraine rambled on as we hurried inside. A waiter approached and quickly placed us at a round table.

"May I suggest today's lunch special? We offer fried pork chops, mashed potatoes and gravy, peas, cornbread, turnip greens and bread pudding."

"Oh my, yes. Sounds good to me." D.A.'s stomach audibly rumbled, and he flushed with embarrassment. "It's been hours since breakfast." He glanced at Lorraine and I, and stifled a laugh.

"You enjoy it, D.A." Lorraine looked at me.

"Sounds delicious, order me the same thing."

Lorraine gave her attention to the waiter. "Three orders of the special."

"And to drink?" The waiter inquired.

We all spoke in unison.

"Iced tea, sweetened."

The waiter left and immediately customers filled the restaurant for the lunch hour. The peaceful atmosphere gave way to constant chatter, chair legs shoved under tables, and loud greetings as some patrons recognized others. Waitresses hurried by carrying large, round platters of meals stacked across their arms. Aromas mingled in the air as the food was dashed off to the correct table.

Lorraine, D.A. and I, watched the hustle and bustle until our order soon arrived. D.A. said grace. The meal's aroma delighted my senses before anyone took the first bite. Silence lingered over the table as we nearly devoured the delectable lunch.

"Thank you both for this meal. Next time, I am buying …right here." I pushed my plate aside and leaned back in the chair.

"You are welcome, and we can all look forwards to eating here again."

I swallowed a long drink of iced tea and noticed a sign in the front window of the restaurant.

"Do you see the sign? I can't read it from here." Squinting at the bright sunshine glaring on the window, I slowly ate another bite of bread pudding.

Lorraine raised her head, cupped a hand over her eyes, and studied the sign. "It says 'Manager Wanted.' Seems like a wonderful job opportunity."

"Business is certainly no problem." D.A. chimed in.

"Wonder what it pays?" I sprang from my chair. "I'll find out. I'm going to the restroom. Be right back." I took off before anyone could respond.

Minutes crawled by until I returned to the table. I slid into my chair with a happy smile.

"Guess what? I heard the job pays almost twice as much as I am making."

"It pays more than your secretary job?" Lorraine widened her eyes.

D.A. sat up straight in his chair. "It does?"

"Yes." I giggled. "It will be perfect. I could walk across the street to go to work. Of course, I don't know anything about being a manager. I don't even know how to waitress."

"You can be taught." Lorraine paused. "You have organizational skills, and you are good with people."

"I think so, too." D. A. nodded.

I glanced around the restaurant with a slow smile spreading across my face.

"I think I can."

Chapter Eight

"I knew you'd get the job." Lorraine placed a bookmark in the current book she was reading and sat upright in the recliner. "Tell me what happened."

I slung my purse onto the end table, plopped onto the couch and stretched out like a cat getting cozy on a soft blanket. I laid my head on a pillow and sighed. "I still can't believe it. I simply walked in, asked for an application, wrote answers to the questions and returned it to the owner. He left me at the counter and took the application with him. It seemed like forever before he rushed back into the room. He said he'd checked out my references, and I am officially hired."

"Did you tell him you are new to this position?"

"Yes. I did, and he said he was willing to train me. He claimed he wanted someone reliable and trustworthy. I also told him I wanted a job description with a list to help me get into a routine. He thought that was a splendid idea, and looked forward to our working together. I can pick up the paperwork this afternoon, get my uniform, and start on Monday."

"Thank the Lord!" Lorraine clapped her hands.

"Amen." I raised my head and lowered my voice. "I gave a silent prayer of thanks as soon as the owner said I was hired."

"And He knows it came from the heart."

"Yes, He does."

"Lil, why don't you rest until this evening? You must be an emotional mess."

"No, I am not jittery. Now that the job is settled, I feel calm and peaceful. I thought I'd catch the bus and go visit Daddy, Bernice, and Raymond for a few hours. Saturday afternoon they are usually home and doing chores."

"Sounds like a plan. Oh, don't forget to write a letter of resignation to your former boss."

"I'll do that now, and hand deliver it to him after church tomorrow. He and his wife attend a Baptist church but live down the street from our Lutheran church. I hope he will understand."

"Pray about it."

"I will." I sprang from the couch "Soon as I finish the letter, I'm off to Daddy's. Want to join us?"

"No, I can't. I have errands to do."

"Anything I can help with?"

"No, but thanks."

"Okay."

I hurried to my room and sat at my desk, staring momentarily at the typewriter. Inserting a blank page, I typed at record speed and completed the task. Upon review, I found no typos. Satisfied, I rushed back to the living room, and snatched my purse off the end table by the couch.

"I'm gone."

"Bye." Lorraine yelled from her bedroom.

Slamming the door behind me, I descended the outside stairs with exuberance. I raced to the bus stop and arrived the same time the bus did. Out of breath, I entered the doors of the bus, stepped up the three rubber-coated steel steps, and deposited the correct amount of change in the machine. Locating an empty seat by a window, I walked down the aisle and promptly sat down as the bus jerked forward.

A people watcher, I discreetly glanced at anyone the bus drove past who happened to be out shopping or merely walking on the sidewalk. Time quickly passed, and I soon recognized my old neighborhood. Drenched by a sudden wave of homesickness, I had a fluttery empty feeling take hold of my stomach. I blinked back tears as thoughts of missing my family intensified.

This is nonsense…I am not a kid anymore…I am twenty years old…

The bus came to a halt, and I departed. Fresh air invigorated me, and today was no exception. Mentally shaking off the homesickness, I made rapid strides to my old street, and approached my family home.

No one knows I'm coming…this will be a happy surprise…

I stepped lightly across the front lawn and tiptoed onto the front porch. Knocking on the screen door, I quickly yelled, "Anyone home?"

Heavy footsteps pounded through the house as shoes and boots raced over the hardwood floors.

"Lilla-Mae, is that you?"

"Yes, it's me, Daddy."

"Girl, look at you... get in here!" He opened the door and pulled me inside. Laughing, I pinched Raymond's cheek, patted Daddy's slight belly, and gave Bernice a hug as they hollered in merriment. "Oh, it's good to be back. Come on, I'm here to help. What chores are you doing?"

"Sister, I am washing cucumbers to pickle." Bernice looked wide-eyed.

"And I'm stuffing jars with dill, garlic, and uh...uh...and pickling spices." Raymond added.

"Sounds like an assembly line." I looked at my younger brother. "Raymond, Daddy's pickles are my favorite. Who's sterilizing the mason jars in boiling water?"

"I am, and you certainly ate your share of pickles." Robert Fritsche smiled.

"I also love to pack the cucumbers into the jars. I'll do that, Daddy. You can pour the hot vinegar over them, and I'll attach the sterilized lids and rings.

"And I'll put the jars back in the pot to boil like I always do."

"Deal."

Raymond and Bernice were experts at their assigned tasks. They had helped for years.

I sat at the table and packed the clean produce into jars and once again, time passed swiftly. I glanced at my father and siblings. "I have some news. I got a job at a restaurant today."

"Lilla-Mae, I am proud of you. That's a blessing to get that job. You will do fine."

"Thanks, Daddy."

"Do we get to eat for free?" Raymond stopped working on the jars and glanced at me.

"No, but I will invite all of you sometime."

Bernice smiled and Raymond nodded. They immediately resumed the pickle assembly line.

An hour later, the jars were boiled and setting on racks to cool. An occasional pop would sound as a jar sealed.

I helped clean the kitchen and turned to leave.

"I've got to pick up my uniform and paperwork at the restaurant this afternoon. I loved our time together, but I have to hurry and catch the bus."

Hugs were exchanged. I grabbed my purse and waved goodbye. Within an hour I had the paperwork and uniform. Arriving home, I discovered Lorraine was still gone. I snuggled into the recliner and read the list detailing my new work routine. Yawning, I blinked as my eyelids seemed heavy, and I drifted off to asleep.

Chapter Nine

"Lil, wake up."

"What?"

"I let you sleep in the recliner last night. I came home late, and you must have been tired. You were slightly snoring."

"Snoring?" I frowned and sprang from the recliner.

"Just a little, come on; breakfast is ready."

I followed my sister to the kitchen where Lorraine had the meal displayed buffet style. Grace was said, and we both grabbed a plate, making selections as Lorraine talked nonstop.

"Just us two this morning, D.A. left for a counseling appointment. I have clothes to wash and iron, so it will be a full day."

I swallowed a bite of scrambled eggs and smiled. "You stay so busy. Let me at least wash the dishes."

"No, scoot along. You want to arrive early for your first day of work."

"Thanks, Lorraine."

"The dishes can soak in the sink until I get a load of clothes washed and hung out on the line."

"Well, I hope you can slow down and rest sometime today. After all, this *is* 1944, not the dark ages."

Lorraine flashed me a smile and disappeared down the hallway.

Today has arrived fast...

I hurried to my room and dressed for work. The uniform of white pants and white shirt was complete with the shirt tucked inside the belted pants. Pivoting in front of the full length mirror behind the bedroom door, I adjusted the shirt for the second time.

"Why not a pale blue color? This uniform won't remain sparkling white with me wearing it…especially around food…"

"Lil, did you say something?"

"Oh, just mumbling to myself…"

"Well, I have clothes to sort. Enjoy your day."

"Thanks."

The door slammed behind Lorraine, echoing through the silent house. I closed the white, metal blinds covering the window. The clicking sound of my white, peep-toe pumps grew louder as I hastened across the hardwood floor.

I can't believe I'm going to be wearing all white around food...

Lil at work

With the morning sunshine blocked, a dim glow cast over the room from the lone, light bulb in the middle of the tall ceiling. I pulled the long, silver chain hanging from the white, porcelain, circle fixture, turned out the light, and said a prayer half-aloud.

Thank You for this job, Lord...and I stand on Your Word... Philippians 4: 13; "I can do all things through Christ who strengthens me..." and my nerves are calmed with You by my side...

Taking a deep breath, I left the house and dashed across the street. Entering the restaurant, I spotted another employee with a name badge and approached her.

"Hi, I'm Lil Fritsche, and…"

The young woman interrupted. "And I've been waiting for you. I'm Emily Ballard." She smiled. "I'll take you to Mr. Solomon's office. He's the owner."

"He interviewed me."

"Mr. Solomon works more like an employee rather than the boss. Here we are." Emily stopped at the office door and knocked.

"Come in." A deep voice boomed.

The young women entered. Mr. Solomon quickly rose from his dark-brown, leather chair and stood behind the massive oak desk.

"Thank you, Emily, you may return to your station. I'll be training Lil today. Lil, welcome, please be seated."

Emily nodded and departed as I slid into a chair facing Mr. Solomon's desk.

He snatched several papers and spread them out in front of me. "Here is this week's work schedule. One of your duties is to insure employers arrive for their shift. A list with their phone numbers and temporary employees to call for emergencies is also available. Later, you will create the schedules yourself."

I scanned each page, and silently noticed eleven employees worked for Mr. Solomon. "I've always been taught to never assume anything about anyone or any situation. Mr. Solomon, do you have some employees more dependable than others?"

"I agree with your statement, and concerning your question, I'd have to say no.

Some have limits and health issues as far as how often they can work. Some have school age children with no baby-sitter. Those employees I schedule for daytime hours. I am flexible."

"I like that, fair treatment…"

"I practice the old saying, 'treat others as you want to be treated.' It makes for a more pleasant day, and a better work environment. Today, I'll show you how to inventory and order supplies. Food is ordered fresh each week. I want you to roam the dining hall as well. You will greet the customers and ask if they need anything else, or if the meal was pleasing. Always be gracious and pleasant, but you should have no problem in that area." He smiled and continued. "Let's go to the kitchen, and I'll introduce you to the staff there." He got up and escorted me to the door.

I caught the scent of homemade yeast rolls as we approached the kitchen through the end of the dining room. Mr. Solomon paused at an occupied table and greeted a customer.

"How is your breakfast this morning?"

"Fine as always, Mr. Solomon. Thank you."

"Thank you, Mr. Sehlke."

"Lil, this is Mr. Sehlke, he is one of our regular customers. Mr. Sehlke, this is Ms. Fritsche, she is our new manager."

"Nice to meet you, ma'am." He turned to face me and smiled.

I glanced at his wavy, light brown hair and looked into his baby-blue eyes, and was overwhelmed. I nodded as my heart pounded in my ears.

What a handsome man…

"Nice to meet you, too." I managed to mumble as Mr. Solomon and I continued to the kitchen.

I turned as we entered through the kitchen door, and the customer accidentally knocked over his water glass as he gazed at me. I caught my breath and tried not to choke.

Chapter Ten

Work days turned into weeks, and I loved the whirlwind of duties at the restaurant. I went to church with Lorraine and D. A., and on this particular Sunday, Daddy, Bernice, and Raymond also came to D.A.'s church to hear him preach.

After the service ended, and the congregation left; my family slowly walked down the steps of the church. The new preacher glanced at his father-in-law, and Robert Fritsche shook his hand.

"Mighty fine sermon, D.A. I'm proud of you."

"Thank you, sir. I'm doing the Lord's work, and give Him the glory."

Daddy nodded and turned towards me. "Speaking of work, how's the new job coming along?"

"Fast-paced, interesting, and I enjoy it."

"Good. You won't get bored, and I heard you even make the work schedules."

Lorraine winked at her sister. "I told Daddy."

"If that's all you told him, then I have news to share."

"It was."

A slow smile appeared on his tired face. "Now, about that news." He glanced at me and crossed his arms.

"I have met someone. His name is Roy."

Roy Sehlke 1945

"Roy? Would I like this Roy?"

"Oh, yes, Daddy. He is a Christian, clean-cut, nice-mannered, handsome, has an Honorable Discharge from the Army…"

"Is he working?"

"Oh my, yes, and he's witty, and thoughtful, and funny, and serious, and wise, and…"

"And he has charmed you, I can tell."

"Yes, he has."

"How did you meet him?"

"He's a regular customer at the restaurant. He wants to take me to the amusement park next Saturday afternoon. I want to go…"

"Then go, have fun. I trust your judgment, Lilla-Mae."

"Thanks, Daddy. I wanted to talk to you about it first. I can't wait to go."

"Well, it sounds like you chose a good man. Of course, this will all be added to my prayers."

I grabbed his hand and squeezed it. "You are in our prayers, also." I whispered.

"Yes, you are." Lorraine added.

Chapter Eleven

Another fast paced week of work sailed by and Saturday arrived. I had left with Roy before lunch, and we spent the day at the carnival. Hours later, I unlocked the front door of D.A. and Lorraine's home and meandered into the kitchen. They were still fully dressed, sitting at the table with each a slice of warm cake, and a glass of cold milk.

Lorraine glanced at the wall clock and blinked. "Home all ready? It's only eight o'clock." She slipped her fork into her slice of cake. Steam escaped, and she slowly blew on it. "Want some? It's a cinnamon coffee cake; I just got it out of the oven."

"It's good, too." D.A. took another bite.

I slid into a chair. "Thanks, but I'm not hungry. We ate too much today. Roy and I sampled food between rides and games until we left the amusement park. Candied apples, caramel popcorn, cotton candy…"

"Sounds like you both enjoyed yourselves."

"Roy kissed me on the Ferris wheel."

"He did what?" Lorraine blurted.

"He put his arm around me as the ride took off, and I clung to the safety bar across my lap. We could see for miles, and it was a breath-taking ride. It stopped going around when we were at the top, and Roy turned to face me and smiled. He quickly kissed me, and the huge Ferris wheel started up and went around again. After the ride ended, we strolled to the bumper cars, and Roy bought tickets for us. We each climbed into a car and zoomed around bumping everyone's car. Every time we crashed into each other, we'd holler. I felt like a teenager. I haven't laughed so much in a long time. Later, we ate hot-dogs, and had lemonade. He even won a stuffed teddy bear for me at a shoot-the-duck arcade. It was fun being with Roy."

"Hmm, your eyes sparkle when you talk about him." Lorraine leaned forward and winked at D.A. "We may have to learn how to spell his last name one day. She may not be Lil Fritsche much longer."

D.A. ducked his head, and I saw the half smile on his face.

"Lorraine, it was only our first date." I sputtered, and felt a warm flush race across my face.

"So…you aren't seeing him soon?"

"Well, yes, we are going on a picnic this coming Saturday, and Roy wants to take me fishing sometime…"

Lorraine swatted lightly at my arm. "I'll stop teasing. I'm just happy for you."

"Thanks." I glanced at her and shook my head. "I think about him constantly. I'll be doing something, and he pops into my thoughts."

"I know what you mean." Lorraine chatted. "Before D. A. and I married, he could say something to me, and I would daydream about it for days."

"And now?" D. A. raised an eyebrow.

"And now I don't have to daydream."

Chapter Twelve

Roy and I dated the entire year of 1946.

Neither of us considered dating others, and we knew our relationship was serious. Returning from a date, we sat on the couch at Lorraine and D.A.'s house when I noticed Roy's sudden nervousness. He glanced at the ceiling, and quickly folded his hands together, popping his knuckles.

"I'd like for you to meet my parents." Roy cleared his throat.

My heart hammered in my chest. "Roy… do you mean…"

"Yes, I want you to marry me." He whispered.

Speechless, I turned my head away from him, smiling at nothing.

Roy's face dampened with perspiration. "I'm waiting…" His voice broke.

I pivoted to face him, no longer calm. "Yes, I will." I sang out.

Caught up in the moment, we hugged tightly, and I gazed into his eyes.

"Roy Sehlke, I am overwhelmed. I could bust wide open, I'm so happy."

He released me and laughed. "Me too, I just waited an eternity for your reply, and I'd already talked to your daddy about it last week."

"You did? What did he say?"

"He said I had his blessing, and that I was the only young man to ever ask for his daughter's hand in marriage."

"Oh, how special. Does he know you want me to meet your parents?"

"Yes. I assured him you would be safe with me. We'd have separate bedrooms at my parents' house and only be gone for a weekend. I even gave him their phone number in Brenham, Texas."

"Thanks, Roy." I paused and considered meeting his parents. "I am nervous about meeting them, though. When do we leave?"

"Tomorrow is Saturday; I'd planned on driving us then. We could return to Houston around noon on Sunday."

"You have certainly been busy planning." I teased. "It's fine with me. I am off work this weekend."

"I know. So, am I." He suddenly poked his hand inside his pants pocket and fidgeted as a red flush crept across his face. Retrieving a small, blue velvet jewelry box, he opened it, and a diamond ring sparkled.

"I nearly forgot."

"Oh, I love it, Roy. A princess cut, it's perfect."

He placed it on my finger and our lips touched lightly in a brief kiss.

"Get to packing, girl." He mumbled and rose from the couch. We strolled arm in arm to the front door where we shared another kiss.

"I'll be back at seven o'clock in the morning. Be ready to go."

"I will." I chuckled as he left. Peeping out the window I watched him skip down the stairs. Alone in the living room, I quickly whirled around and squealed with joy.

~~##~~

I yawned and glanced for the hundredth time out the window at the isolated farms. Each appeared miles from the highway as a tiny dot surrounded by vast acreage. The countryside was crisscrossed with barb-wire wooden fences, and the different crops swayed gently in the early morning breeze.

"Pleasant. Roy, it looks like a pleasant, story-book illustration. We lived on a farm before but with more trees."

"We lived in town. Mom and Pop always had a garden, still do. Mom even has a fenced area with geese. Talk about mean, they will chase you squawking and spreading their clipped wings. Loud, too." Roy winked and gave me a sly smile. "Nothing better than a baked goose for Thanksgiving."

"They are good." I sat silently for several miles.

Roy stole a glance at me and quickly returned his focus to the road.

"Why the frown?"

"Am I frowning? Guess I was just lost in thought, I do that sometimes."

"I know you do. What's on your mind?"

"Oh, thinking about meeting your parents. I'm getting jittery. Hope I don't spill something or…"

Roy interrupted. "You will be fine. Relax."

"Thanks."

"There's the Brenham city limits sign."

"Didn't seem to take long. How many miles is it from Houston, anyway?"

"About 80 miles."

Roy exited the highway and carefully weaved into local traffic. "We are almost in their neighborhood. They live near downtown a block down and across the street from a Catholic Church. You will enjoy hearing the bells ring from the belfry tomorrow morning."

He zipped through the quiet streets, and I sighed.

"I am already relaxed. It's so peaceful here." I suddenly sat upright and stared through the windshield. "Roy, look at the group of nuns walking down the sidewalk. I'll never forget the sight of them in their long, black habits...like they are floating along."

"The nuns do look serene. I personally don't believe in the Catholic faith, and I know you don't either. The Bible doesn't say a mortal man, a priest, can forgive you of your sins. Only our Heavenly Father through Jesus can forgive us of our sins, and the Bible doesn't say for us to pray to Jesus' mother Mary. I will not call a mortal man Father, unless it's my birth Father, and I only have one Heavenly Father. A priest is not my father."

"I agree."

He pulled into his parent's driveway, and I felt butterflies in my stomach. Without realizing what I was doing, I clutched my fingers onto the edge of the seat. Roy glanced at the grip I had on the car seat, and his voice softened.

"Are you going to be okay with meeting them?"

"Yes, I am." I blurted out too fast, and paused. "I love their home."

"Okay."

I looked again at the house. The distinguished Craftsman house was red brick with white pillars, a wide front porch, and white lattice underpinning three feet high. The front door swung open, and a man walked out with a slight limp, followed by a short, stout, middle-aged woman.

"Dad's name is Oscar Julius Sehlke, and he hurt his back in the oil-fields, that's why he limps…"

"Oh, how awful for him."

"…and Mom's name is Martha, she's a great cook…that's why she is kind of heavy." He grinned.

"She probably wouldn't like you saying that." Mischievous, I relaxed and felt more comfortable.

"Ever play musical chairs where a few walk round a smaller amount of chairs, and when the music stops you try to sit in a chair and someone is left out?"

"Yes."

"Well get ready for musical hugs without the music."

I raised my eyebrows at him. "Your family hugs?"

"Trust me."

We left the vehicle and hurried across the lawn and up the brick steps to the porch.

"Mom, Pop, this is Lil, your future daughter-in-law."

"Welcome to our home." Martha Sehlke stepped forward and lightly embraced me, patting me gently on the back.

"Thank you."

Oscar Sehlke promptly grabbed me from Martha's embrace, and gave me a heart-felt hug. "Glad to meet you, Lil."

"You too sir, both of you."

Roy quickly hugged his mom as Oscar released me.

"Son, you did well. She is a beauty." He slapped Roy on the shoulder.

Roy instantly left his mom and hugged his dad. Martha ambled to the front door, and I glanced at her with a shy smile.

"Well, come inside, you two. Let's get situated." Martha held the elaborated carved, wooden door open, and we entered.

Roy laughed. "I think we're all hugged out."

Roy's parents: Oscar & Martha Sehlke

I immediately noticed the impressive furnishings in the spotlessly clean home, and the many collections displayed in lighted curio cabinets. Martha waved an arm at one of them when I lingered in front it.

"I had two sons and no daughters. This is my collection of dolls. I like the small porcelain dolls wearing dresses with the large, billowing skirts worn during the plantation era of the civil war. Some dolls are dressed in silk clothes, others in crochet or polished cotton." She paused and turned towards me. "Of course, no one is allowed to play with them."

"Oh, I won't touch them. You have a magnificent collection."

"Thank you." Martha said and ushered us into the dining room. "Please be seated. I am cooking breakfast. It won't be but a few more minutes."

Again, she waved her arm. This time at the table completely set with plates, glasses, silverware and linens.

"Can I help you?" I made eye contact with Martha.

"No, it's nearly done."

Martha hastened through an adjoining door, and Roy grabbed my arm. "Let's sit on this side of the table, and they can sit across from us."

Easing into chairs, conversation flowed as Martha returned with plates mounded high with bacon, scrambled eggs, homemade yeast rolls, and jellies. Ice cold milk was poured, and Oscar said the blessing. The meal was almost wiped out in less than ten minutes.

"Breakfast was delicious, Mom." Roy wiped his mouth with the linen napkin.

"Thank you, Mrs. Sehlke. It was wonderful. Can I help you clear the table?"

"No, I'll do that, and I'm glad you both enjoyed it." She shot Oscar a stern look as he continued spreading butter and jelly on another yeast roll.

The gesture was lost on Oscar though. He poured himself another glass of milk and slowly took another bite of the warm roll. Martha stared at her husband in obvious contempt.

Roy quickly held his hand under his nose, attempting to rub the area and almost managed to hide the sudden grin on his face.

Puzzled, I cautiously gave him a slow, half smile.

"Lil, let's go to the back yard. There is something I want to show you."

"Okay." I sprang from my chair and followed Roy outside. Escaping, we left Oscar to face Martha's anger alone.

Geese instantly approached the side of their pen that faced us. Squawking and raising their clipped wings, they got as close to us as possible. We had intruded upon their fenced area and decided we needed to stop and talk to them. They made eye contact, stuck out their necks and squawked back at us excitedly. It was a fun moment. We eventually left their area, meandering by flowerbeds and manicured shrubbery. Roy snickered as Martha's loud, sharp words to Oscar sailed out the kitchen window for all to hear. Apparently, she wanted the remaining rolls to be served later with dinner. Mumbled chatter ensued and peace returned.

Roy nodded at me, and we nonchalantly proceeded back to the house. He picked a rose near the entrance and once inside, offered it to his mother. She smiled sweetly.

"Where's Dad?"

"Watching television in the living room, a ball game starts in a few minutes."

He left me in the kitchen with his mother and joined his dad. Martha turned her back to me and bent over the sink washing dishes.

"Oh, let me help you." I pleaded.

"No." The word spat out as her voice took on a sudden harshness.

I cringed and lightly stepped closer. "Please, I just want to help."

Martha's back visibly stiffened. I gasped when I noticed Martha was washing the dishes without using soap. She held them under hot, running water and wiped them with a dishcloth.

"You're not using soap." I muttered and looked down.

"No, I'm not. I'm out of soap." Martha kept her back to me.

"I'm sorry. I shouldn't have said anything. I was just so shocked."

Martha fell silent, and I waited for her to finish the task. Silence grew heavy in the room, and I finally fled to the living room.

The evening hours seemed to increase the distance between myself and Martha. No attempt at any conversation I made was warmly received by her. Roy and his dad discussed the neighbors, Roy's fellow classmates, his childhood adventures, and included me in their stories and laughter. Martha solemnly served dinner and later, showed Roy and I to each one's bedroom for the night. Oscar helped us remove our overnight bags from the car, and everyone went to bed as Martha hurried to turn out the lights.

The next morning, I awoke to hear the church bells ringing and as they rang out, I immediately felt compelled to pray for Martha.

Lord, Martha is heavy on my mind. Please forgive anything I might have said or done to cause the bitterness emitted from Roy's mother. I pray for your love and peace to surround her and melt her cold heart. This whole weekend has me missing my own mother again...why is Martha so harsh? Lord. I pray for this family and for Your will to be done. In Jesus powerful name I pray, Amen.

Martha's posture was erect, and her words were brisk and clipped to everyone that morning. After breakfast, Roy and I climbed back in the car as goodbyes were said.

Leaving Brenham, I involuntarily shivered in the car and glanced at Roy. "I don't think your mother likes me."

"Nonsense. She has her own way of doing things. It's just how she is. Pop and I have to get out of her way sometimes." He laughed.

We chatted and arrived at Lorraine and D.A.'s house a little over an hour later. The phone was ringing when we entered.

Roy stood by my side as I answered it, and I listened to the caller without interrupting.

"Oh, that's great news. Okay, I can't wait." I hung up the receiver and giggled.

"That was Bernice who just phoned; she has a job interview at Weingarten's."

Roy held two thumbs up, and his mouth stretched into a happy straight line. He quickly kissed my upturned face and crossed his arms over his chest. "And we, my dear, have wedding plans to make."

I laughed and briefly closed my eyes. "I can already picture it."

Chapter Thirteen

"Miss Fritsche, you are hired."

Bernice beamed. "Thank you, sir. When do I start?"

"You'll work Monday from 8 am to 5 pm with Mrs. Myer in the deli. She will train you. I'll get your uniforms, and a schedule." He spoke in a professional business manner, and bustled to a nearby supply closet retrieving a stack of uniforms. "They come in small, medium, and large. I am guessing you wear a medium." He looked first at Bernice, and then glanced at a large wall calendar covered with hand-written notes.

"Yes, medium will be fine."

He handed her three uniforms and added her name to the scheduled work calendar. Scribbling a note, he pivoted towards her.

"Here's your work week. Welcome to Weingarten's Grocery."

"Thanks again." Bernice calmly retrieved the note and shook his hand. Overwhelmed with the sudden realization of having the job, she felt her pulse race and managed to squelch her excitement. A solemn nod to her employer, and she left the office. Quick to depart the store, she caught the next bus and bounced up the steps, pausing to throw coins in the meter. Her fare paid, she scanned the rows of passengers and found an unoccupied seat. Leaning her head back, she took a deep breath.

I got the job…my first job… thank you Lord!

Her fingers lightly danced across her knees keeping rhythm with the song she and the choir would soon be practicing for tomorrow's Sunday service. Arriving at her destination fifteen minutes later, Bernice hummed a tune and rushed inside the church.

The heavy, wooden door made a loud groaning noise upon her entrance followed by a refreshing blast of fresh air.

I stood with the choir behind Mr. Koch. He was in front of the podium. All singers raised their heads from the sheet music they each held as Bernice entered.

"Lil, I got the job." Bernice yelled and ran to me.

I bolted down the aisle. Grabbing ahold of Bernice, I quickly hugged her.

"I'm happy for you, sister. What a great Saturday this turned out to be for all of us."

Bernice, momentarily perplexed, frowned at me. "Has something else happened?"

"Yes, Roy and I are to marry here on December 15th, and I want you to be my maid of honor."

"Oh, Lil, I'm happy for you and Roy, and I'm proud to be your maid of honor. Imagine, getting married here at our church…"

I interrupted. "Thank you, sister, and I know what you're thinking. You're wondering if I'm ready."

Bernice took the hint and happily sang from an old spiritual song we often harmonized.

"Are you ready, my sister?"

"Oh yes." I sang back.

"Are you ready for the journey?" Bernice continued singing.

"Oh yes. I'm ready for the journey, and I'm ready to go." I responded in song.

Our voices joined together, "I never will forget the day, Jesus took my sins away. My Lord, my Lord…ready to see my Lord."

Joyful, we walked to the loft for an hour of choir practice.

~~##~~

The song, 'Are You Ready My Sister' became a daily part of mine and Bernice's greeting to each other. Upon saying hello, after receiving a phone call from the other, one would sing the familiar words, 'Are you ready my sister?' and the other would sing 'oh yes' with equal excitement as we sang the rest of the song. This sweet greeting continued exclusively between the us two sisters for the rest of our lives.

Chapter Fourteen

Love this quiet morning…no work today and Lorraine and D.A. are gone…

I slipped my needle through the material and was pleased with my embroidery work. The pattern was a forest scene printed on a narrow table runner with a white background. I'd outlined the deer in brown, and the trees in green. It was relaxing and nearly complete.

A loud, sudden pounding interrupted my pleasure, and I flinched.

Who can be here this early?

Laying my sewing aside on the couch, I rushed to open the front door, and stood facing my older sister, Amanda.

"What a surprise, Amanda, how are you?"

"I am well, thank you, and congratulations. News of your upcoming wedding is racing through the family. Everyone is delighted you are marrying Roy."

"Thank you. I've received phone calls from siblings, friends, and people I haven't seen in years. Come inside." I ushered her in to the living room. She plopped down on the love seat, and I returned to the couch.

"I imagine you are happily making plans."

"I have sorted through a lot of ideas, but no, I haven't made any definite decisions on anything. There are tons of details to consider and finalize. I'm glad the wedding is a few months away."

"That's why I'm here. I want to help. When is the exact date?"

"December, 15th, this year, 1946. Can you believe it's already 1946? I feel like Roy and I have dated forever. Oh, yes, Amanda, I would love having your help."

"Wonderful. We'll start by moving you in with me at my house."

"Your house? I don't mind, in fact I'd enjoy that, but why your house?"

"Lorraine and D.A.'s house is too far away from our church. I'm sure you want to be married in the church you grew up in with everyone you know."

"Of course, I do."

"And I think you should quit your job. It will involve too much travel time from my house, and our time together needs to be more productive. If it's okay with you, I'd like to start immediately discussing and completing your wedding plans."

"I would like that. Amanda, it will be a relief to have every detail approved and scheduled."

"What do you intend to do with Roy's parents during the wedding?"

"I hadn't thought of that."

"I will offer a room to them. I have a three bedroom house. My spare bedroom has an adjoining bathroom they could use. They could arrive one day early for the wedding, and leave when it's over."

"If they will agree to those arrangements, I think it is noble of you to accommodate them. I'll talk to Roy, and let him ask his parents. He has a one bedroom apartment, and it would be impossible for them to stay with him. I like your suggestion."

"Well, that's taken care of." Amanda leaned back in the love seat putting her hands behind her head. "If we were making a list, the next item would be to quit your job."

I slumped down on the couch and felt my chest tighten. Reality set in. I felt overwhelmed. I loved my job and would miss everyone there. "I want to give at least two weeks' notice to my employer."

"Two weeks maximum. You are getting married, remember? You also have a wedding dress to select. They will understand, and I'm sure they already appreciate the values you display by your work."

I knew she was right and meant well. Being at a loss for words, I nodded.

"Back to the wedding, I guess I don't have to ask who your maid of honor will be."

"Bernice." I chuckled, and excitement returned as I pictured the big day.

"She could almost be your daughter."

"Yes, and I appreciate you, Amanda, for taking the role that my mother would have had in preparing for my wedding."

"Oh, Lil, I am honored to help, and I forgot to tell you what Elsie wants to do."

"I figured Elsie would help, too. What does she have in mind?"

"Our sister wants to have the reception at her house after the wedding."

"Oh, how nice, I would love it," I exclaimed and leaped off the couch. Giving Amanda a big hug, I felt my knees weaken.

Overcome with emotion, I knew what I blessing my family was to me.

She left and once again, I found myself writing another letter to an employer submitting my two weeks' notice to resign. The days of work at the restaurant went by fast. Amanda was correct; everyone at the restaurant understood why I had to leave, thought I was a great employee and co-worker, and were encouraging about my upcoming wedding.

I moved in with Amanda, and got caught up in a whirlwind of activities. The rehearsal dinner was selected, and the flowers, bridesmaids' dresses, and my gifts were chosen. Next came my wedding dress, decorations for the church, food at Elsie's house and decorations there, as well. My family paid for everything.

Roy's parents agreed to spend the night at Amanda's house for the wedding. They would arrive by bus. Roy would meet them at the bus station and drive them to Amanda's.

After the wedding, Amanda would take them back to catch the bus, and they would return to Brenham, Texas.

December 15th, finally arrived. Our wedding was beautiful. Many pictures were taken, and Roy and I couldn't stop smiling. It was such a special day. I'll never forget walking down the aisle in the church with the organ playing, and how happy we all were. Amanda left shortly after the wedding to take Roy's parents to her home. They packed, and Amanda drove them to the bus station.

Lil's sister Amanda, sister Bernice, Lil, & sister Elsie on Lil's wedding day; Dec. 15, 1946.

The reception went well at my sister Elsie's house. Guests filled her home and stayed for hours. It was the custom for the groomsmen or someone to take the groom away after the wedding at the reception. In our case, it was my brothers. Roy was not aware of this custom. My brothers grabbed him while they were outside and drove off with him. They kept him about an hour before returning. My sisters knew what was going on, and were all laughing when the guys came back with

Roy. He seemed nervous, and I felt sorry for him. It did end up okay, though, with Roy. Everything went smoothly after that episode.

No other surprises until we arrived at Roy's apartment later that night. My same brothers got involved in another custom. They managed to get inside the apartment, and 'short changed' the sheets on the bed. When we pulled back the chenille bedspread, we couldn't get our feet very far in the bed. The top sheet had been pulled out from underneath the bottom of the mattress, and brought up half-way to the top of the bed. When we crawled into the bed, between the sheets, our feet would only go half way down the mattress. Roy thought it was funny, and I was embarrassed. We had to take the sheets off, and make the bed the normal way. After that, we were both leery of everything else in the apartment.

    We were entirely too crowded at the apartment and soon bought a house. I obtained a job at a local bakery near our neighborhood, and life was good.

Roy and I continued spending the day fishing on the coast whenever we could. We loved the outing. Sometimes, Roy and I didn't have off work on the same day, and Roy would go fishing with my sister Marie's husband, Otto. It was not unusual for them to return with burlap sacks full of oysters along with a bucket or two of fish. The men would shuck oysters in our garage for hours, and the four of us would enjoy the oysters with a fish fry that evening. Yum! We loved fresh seafood.

We would even camp out on the beach with my married brothers and their wives; and my married sisters with their husbands. Not all came at the same time. Whoever could go would do so, and we began a tradition of singing around the campfire, while some fished, and others cooked. It was fun, and everyone looked forwards to it. I was blessed with a great family. No one had bad health, and no one was too old to participate.

Bernice was the next member of our family to marry. She and her husband Jimmy were married in our church, and I was her matron of honor. Our entire family attended the wedding, and it was another happy moment.

Roy and I continued to enjoy our life together, and our home.

Roy & Lil 1947

Chapter Fifteen

Roy opened the back door and poked his head inside the kitchen. "Come on out, we have radishes."

The good news he shared may not seem important to anyone else, but it did to me. Progress on the garden we'd laughed and labored over was a rewarding moment, indeed. The fact that he included me in whatever he did, outside of his job, melted my heart. I loved our married life.

Smiling at his handsome, tanned face, I threw the dishcloth onto the recently washed breakfast dishes. Drying them could wait.

Roy made a beeline to the garden, and I made rapid strides to keep up with him. The garden covered over half of our back yard. Each row was straight, and not one weed could be found.

"They are popping up quick." He squatted and pointed to the tiny, green plants protruding from the ground.

"I've never seen thick clusters of them in a long row."

"I'll have to thin them out, later."

"I'll help."

Roy stood and wiped his brow. It was only eight o'clock, and the heat from the morning sun had steadily increased since he'd removed weeds earlier. He retrieved the hoe leaning against the fence and chopped at grass near the edge of the last row. "We'll wait until they are larger."

I scanned the rest of the rows and admired the results.

"Looking good, Mr. Sehlke, mighty good. Corn is growing tall, cabbages are heading, peas are climbing, tomatoes and squash are blooming; I could go on and on."

"Thank you, Mrs. Sehlke." He winked. "I think we're done here for today."

"Sea breeze calling your name?"

"Yes ma'am. I'll load the fishing gear, and you can pack our lunch."

"Will do. I love Thursdays. I feel like your one day off a week is my only day off, too."

Roy & Lil fishing in Galveston, Texas

Laughter filled the air as we fled the garden. Galveston, Texas was less than an hour's drive from the home we'd bought in Houston. Each Thursday was spent with an enjoyable fishing trip to either Galveston, or Kemah, Texas.

Waves lapped at the sides of the rented boat, and I re-tied the long cords from my straw hat into a bow with a knot. Tight against the underneath of my chin, the straw hat was snug but secure. Brisk wind sailed about, and the brim of the hat flopped up and down.

Another gust covered us with a heavy mist of sea water. I sputtered at the salty taste and held onto the seat as the boat dipped into a shallow wave.

A huge smile appeared on Roy's face as he cast his line out into the ocean.

"I've got a bite," I exclaimed, and reeled the fish towards the boat. My line jerked as the fish thrashed in the water.

Roy reached and grabbed the line. "Here, I've got it." He pulled the fish out, and removed the hook, dumping yet another red snapper inside the bucket.

"Your face is getting a bit sunburned, babe. Let's stop and have lunch."

I nodded, and laid my rod and reel on the bottom of the boat. Roy did the same, moved to sit close to the motor, and tried to start it. After several attempts, the motor cranked and roared alive. We sped off to locate a bridge, or a tall public dock.

"I don't think we're going to find a shady spot today." I hollered over the noise of the brand new, 1946 Evinrude outboard motor. The sun's rays bore down from the cloudless sky and glistened over the water as we both scanned the horizon.

We continued until spotting a shoreline dotted with boats, buildings, and short piers. Eventually, a long pier jutted out towards us.

Roy slowed his approach and dropped anchor near the support beams. Activity flourished onshore, but at the end of this pier, we had a secluded and peaceful, picnic area.

Prepared, I unpacked items from the picnic basket to clean our hands. I placed homemade sandwiches wrapped in paper napkins on our laps, and we shared a bag of potato chips. Roy pulled two bottles of Coca-Cola from the side of a block of ice in the red, metal, Army Coca-Cola cooler, and handed one to me.

"I can't believe you've got this cooler. It even has a bottle opener on the side."

"I was in the Army. One of my buddies sent it to me from Germany earlier this year. I can't believe how cold this bottle of coke is." Munching heartily, the meal was consumed quickly.

"Roy…" I hesitated and waited as he gulped the last swallow of his drink.

"What?" He looked wide-eyed at me.

"You know how close Bernice and I are?"

"I know, and she and Jimmy had a nice wedding two weeks ago. I am happy for them."

"So am I…"

"And?"

"And Bernice wants them to move in with us, if it's okay. They could have their own bedroom."

"Are you joking?"

"No."

"He's not abusing her, is he?"

I gasped. "Oh, no, of course not."

"In that case; she is now a married woman, and her place is with her husband."

"I agree, but remember, I am the only Mother she ever had. I raised her. She misses me."

Roy chuckled, and the tone of his voice lightened. "It's fine with me."

Lil clasped his hand and squeezed it. "Thank you. I'll call her as soon as we get home."

"We'll have to move some furniture around. Guess we'd better get going."

"Thanks again." I threw the remains of lunch back inside the picnic basket, and Roy cranked the Evinrude.

He turned to face me. "Hold on," he yelled.

We both hunkered down in the boat and zoomed away.

Chapter Sixteen

"Lil, where are they?"

"Outside. Bernice washed clothes, and Jimmy carried the basket of wet laundry for her. She's hanging them on the clothesline."

Roy took a deep breath and exhaled loudly. "It's been three months, time for them to find their own place. We are too crowded, and they can afford an apartment. They are grown adults."

"Bernice has always been a large part of my life. I don't want to hurt her feelings."

"Have you talked to them about moving?"

"Sort of..." I grimaced "Bernice is so in love with Jimmy...she thinks he is perfect. She said anyone would enjoy being in his company and can't imagine them ever leaving here. She is content..."

"Bernice is your sister. You have to talk to her. I love them both, but it's for the best, Lil. We can't all continue to live in a little, two bedroom home with only one bathroom."

"I understand." My shoulders suddenly slumped. Silently, I left the house. Proceeding through the back yard to the clothesline, I noticed Jimmy talking to a neighbor through the chain-link fence. Bernice pulled a sheet from the basket and struggled to shake it.

"Here, let me help." I took a corner, and Bernice held the other. Together we popped the sheet in the air, and secured it on the line with wooden clothes pins.

"Much easier, thanks." Bernice bent over the basket, and retrieved a towel. I scooted the clothes pin basket further towards us on the line.

"Bernice, I need to talk to you about something."

"What about?"

"You know how we are always bumping into each other? It's like this house is getting smaller and smaller, and the chores keep growing larger and larger. Washing dishes, cleaning the floors, cleaning the tiny bathroom and the commode…"

"I agree, but what about the commode?" Bernice frowned.

I looked Bernice straight in the face and lowered my voice. "Bernice, you don't clean it, and your husband uses it too. Someone is occasionally leaving a few drops on the outside front of the pot."

Bernice's frown deepened. She instantly dropped the towel back into the basket and promptly placed both hands on her sides. "Are you saying something against Jimmy? Roy uses that commode, too."

"No, Bernice. We could take turns cleaning it. If you and Jimmy continue to stay here, you are going to have to share the chores."

"Don't worry about the commode. Jimmy has been telling me that we need to find an apartment. So, it looks like we will be finding one soon."

"It's not all about the commode, but I'm sure going to miss you, honey."

"I know, and I am going to miss you. I love you so much."

"I love you too, Bernice, you are just like my daughter, and always will be."

~~##~~

Unfortunately, it took Bernice getting mad about the commode for them to leave. They found an apartment and moved out that same week. We never mentioned the commode again. The following summary explains that she didn't stay mad at me long.

Roy and I had our first daughter in December, 1948. Bernice later became pregnant and was scared of being left alone while Jimmy was at work. They moved back in with Roy and I until their baby son was born. Jimmy's mother, Ruby, insisted they move in with her when the hospital released Bernice, so she could help Bernice with the baby. They did. Their son was born in January, 1951.

Ruby was controlling with the baby. She wouldn't let Bernice bathe the baby, and insisted on holding or rocking him to sleep. She hovered over him constantly, ignoring Bernice's pleas to stop. After a few weeks of this treatment; Bernice, Jimmy, and the baby moved in with Roy and I and our daughter. They remained until their baby son was one year old. At that time, Jimmy and Bernice bought a house and moved permanently.

I invited them over each Sunday for dinner, and this became a tradition with our two families. I loved it; after all, I was the only Mother she ever had.

Chapter Seventeen

When Roy and I had our first baby, a little girl; we'd been married for two years. We named our daughter, Jayne Lynn, (pronounced Janie) and were thrilled. The first time the nurse brought the baby to me in the hospital, I was in the room alone. I held my daughter close in my arms, and then laid her on my lap. I counted and played with her fingers and toes and marveled out loud how perfect she was. Overwhelmed with love, I kissed her cheek and gazed into her face.

"You are all mine. You don't belong to any of my big sisters, not one of them. You are all mine, honey."

I heard something and glanced up. My doctor was standing in the doorway, smiling. I don't know how long he had been standing there, but he seemed as happy as I was.

"That makes the past hours' worth it, doesn't it?"

"Yes, it does. I can forget the hard labor pains. Now, it seems like they only lasted a few minutes. And I have to laugh at when my husband brought me here several days ago. Other woman were moaning and hollering in pain so loud that it scared me. My pains quit, and I had my husband take me home. We didn't know it then, but I was having false labor pains."

"And here she is, born on Christmas day." Dr. Hall exclaimed.

"Yes, she's born on the very day we celebrate the birth of our Lord and Savior, Jesus Christ." I paused, and looked at the baby again.

"Yes ma'am."

I glanced at the doctor. "Out of the fifteen brothers and sisters I have, my daddy only came to the hospital to see my baby. He didn't go see any of theirs. It makes my Christmas that much more special."

"It is a special day, Mrs. Sehlke. Merry Christmas to you."

"Merry Christmas to you, also, Dr. Hall."

~~##~~

When Jayne was only seven months old, she started walking. It was remarkable because she was so little. I would dress her in pinafores or a lacy dress, take the city bus, and let her walk on the sidewalks in downtown Houston. Everyone remarked on how little she was to be walking, and how cute she was. I, of course, just beamed, and was so proud to show her off …even to strangers.

Bernice sewed the cutest dresses for Jayne, and after she had her son, we'd often take our children out in public together. Her little boy, Jimmy Ray, also wore clothes that Bernice made. She enjoyed selecting patterns and ended up with a sewing room full of material.

Years later, Roy and I took Jayne with us on our fishing trips to Galveston, Texas. It was a busy and happy family time for us.

I became pregnant with my second daughter, Rhonda Kay, about the same time Bernice became pregnant with her second son, Steve.

One day, my neighbor, Delores, phoned me and was almost out of breath.

"Lil, a taxi-cab just pulled up and parked in front of your house. You need to check it out."

"How unusual," I replied. "Thanks for telling me." I hung up the receiver and went to look out the living room window facing the street.

There she was.

Bernice.

She was enormous… eight months pregnant. Standing next to the taxi-cab, she had one hand holding little Jimmy Ray's hand, and the other hand holding her suitcase.

"Oh no." I groaned.

I ran out of the house to her, and the taxi-cab drove off.

"Jimmy made me mad, and I left him." She blurted. Her face turned red as she marched towards me.

"Oh, Bernice…" I grabbed the suitcase from her, and she stopped walking and picked up little Jimmy Ray. She carried him on her side over her hip. He looked wide-eyed at her, and she made a silly face. He laughed and relaxed. She turned to me.

"Jimmy said something about not getting breakfast, and I can't help having morning sickness. I don't have to take that from him. He went to work, and I left."

"Bernice, honey, talk to him about it first. Try to work this out another way…there has to be another way that will work for both of you."

"I don't know…"

We reached the front door of my house, and I escorted them in to the kitchen. We chatted awhile, and I managed to calm her down.

"You have to go home, Bernice. Jimmy loves you, and you know it."

She sighed and finally gave in. "I know."

Late that afternoon, she phoned Jimmy at work and asked him to come and pick her up. She said she was at my house, had become tired, and didn't think she could take a bus ride home.

He arrived; dashing and charming, handsome with his dark mop of hair.

"Is my baby girl, okay?" He showered Bernice with sweet words of concern. She was mesmerized and smiled at me as they left.

Roy and I took the suitcase back to her the next Thursday. Jimmy never knew she had left him.

Chapter Eighteen

The problem with my right ear had worsened over the years. I avoided slowing down and tried to continue my busy life. My happiness was being a wife and Mother.

In 1954, I felt labor pains as my second baby's birth neared, and shrugged them off. I remembered Roy taking me to the hospital when I had Jayne. The moaning women in labor had scared me. I ended up having false labor pains, and Roy had to take me back to our home. I had Jayne a week later.

I wasn't going to go through that again.

Roy was at work so I phoned my sister, Marie.

"I think I am having false labor pains."

"Lil, the second baby comes faster. You need to go on to the hospital."

"No. Roy is at work, anyway. I am going to wait."

"I'm telling you not to wait. Otto has off work today, and he can take you. I'm sending Otto over now. He will drive you to the hospital."

We hung up the phone, and I was annoyed with Marie. I didn't want my brother-in-law rushing me off to the hospital when it wasn't hard labor pains.

Otto arrived, and grabbed my suitcase. We hurried to the hospital, and I sat in the waiting room glancing at a magazine. Otto took off to the admitting desk, and a nurse followed him to where I calmly sat.

"Ma'am, you need to sit in this wheel chair, and I'll wheel you up to the third floor."

"Okay," I sighed and complied with her request.

I was prepped and sent to the delivery room. Within minutes Rhonda Kay was born. Marie was right. I thanked her and Otto later. Roy came to see us when he got off of work.

Rhonda was a perfect baby. She was beautiful, of course. She would lie in her crib, and look around the room, content and adorable. Rhonda never cried. I would pick her up, and hug her, and she cooed at me. I was thrilled to have two daughters.

My five year old daughter, Jayne, considered herself to be a 'big girl' and was the constant companion of baby Rhonda. One day I had to go outside to hang laundry on the clothesline, and both girls were wide awake.

No doing chores while they nap, today…

"Jayne, watch your sister. Don't let her roll off the pallet."

"I won't." Sincere, she stood nearby guarding the baby. I gripped the heavy basket of wet laundry with both hands, veered towards the back door, and inched across the back yard to the clothesline. Listening intently while I hung clothes on the line, the silence I noticed was reassuring. Ten minutes later I entered the house, and it was still quiet. No crying. No hollering, just blissful peacefulness. Walking into the kitchen I was surprised not to find baby Rhonda where I had left her. Jayne happily strolled in from the living room with her arm encircled around the baby's head. Rhonda hung down from Jayne's grasp with a pleasant smile on her face.

I darted toward Jayne and carefully retrieved my baby.

"Jayne, you can't carry her around like that. It could hurt her."

"Okay, Mama." She blinked her eyes and ran outside to play.

The following week, the same situation of having chores to complete with wide awake daughters happened again, but this time I decided not to take any chances. I tied Rhonda into the high chair so Jayne couldn't carry her around while I hung clothes outside.

"Jayne, you can watch the baby, but don't carry her around."

"I won't carry her around, Mama." Jayne answered sweetly.

I returned as quickly as possible and found baby Rhonda out of the high chair and lying on a pallet.

"Jayne, what did you do?" I scolded.

"Mama, she was wiggling, and I made her a pallet. She likes the pallet."

I sighed and vowed not to leave them alone again. After that, Roy hung the laundry on the clothesline when he came home from work, and it stayed outside all night. One of us retrieved it the next day while the other watched the two girls.

A few weeks later, Roy installed training wheels on Jayne's bicycle. She loved riding up and down the concrete driveway. She knew not to get on the street and always minded our rules.

"Mama, can I ride my bicycle awhile?" She asked one morning while I washed dishes. It was early in the day and not too hot outside.

"Yes, but stay on the driveway. Be careful."

Her face lit up with excitement. "I will, Mama," she called out joyfully as she sailed out the door.

Her screams were almost instant upon going outside. They startled me and I ran, heart pounding, outside to my daughter. There to my horror lay Jayne on the ground with a huge dog on top of her mauling, nonstop. I screamed, and ran to her waving my arms, trying to shoo the dog away. Delores and her husband, my next door neighbors, came running and Delores's husband kicked the dog off Jayne. I gathered her in my arms, and the dog ran off. We took her to the hospital and were informed she had to have shots, one daily for twenty-one days to prevent rabies because it was a stray animal. She was stitched up and released. I held her and cried.

Each day going to get a shot was a nightmare for all of us, especially Jayne. No matter what route we took, she'd scream, and after a few days she would balk at entering the car. It seemed forever before the ordeal was over. It was months before I'd let her outside without me by her side. Even with that precaution, she'd scan the yard to insure it was safe. It took a while, and she returned to her old self…the big girl who could handle anything.

I experienced headaches and dizziness more often, and shooting pains in my ears. I suddenly lost all hearing in my right ear a week later. An appointment with an eye, ear, nose, and throat specialist resulted in having a mastoid ear operation scheduled for my right ear. Due to a cancellation, my surgery waiting time went from four weeks to one week. I was anxious to have it done, and get it over with, so the healing could begin. After all, it was 1956, and I trusted the expertise of my doctor.

The surgery lasted over an hour. After I came out of recovery, the doctor entered my room, and he was shaking. He told me he removed a lot, and I now had a huge cavity inside my head. He explained he came within the width of a hair from my brain. I was not to let any water get in that ear. He kept shaking as he talked. I listened as he told me I had a week to live. It took a moment for me to realize what he was saying. I sucked my breath in and choked, coughing in panic. I exhaled. He kept talking on and on.

A week to live…no…dear Lord…no…

Still lying in the hospital bed, I quickly turned my head to face the wall. Adrenaline rushed through my body, and I immediately thought of my children. Emitting a low moan, my stomach knotted up, and I trembled. Stress was making a wreck out of me.

No… I can't accept his diagnose…dear Lord…help me through this…

I felt the doctor pat me on my shoulder, and he called to a nurse in the hall to bring me a wheelchair.

Turning his attention back to me, I heard compassion in his voice. "Do you want something to help you sleep?"

"No, thank you. The pain medication is enough. I'd rather be alert."

"I have your discharge papers ready, Mrs. Sehlke. Rest when you get home. Call me if I can be of any help."

I nodded at the doctor. He left. The nurse arrived with a wheel chair and gathered my belongings.

Roy entered the room, pale and quiet. His presence comforted me, and he squeezed my hand. The nurse suggested Roy bring the car around to the front of the hospital while she wheeled me to the elevator. He took off. She and I slowly made our way to the downstairs lobby and met Roy. He helped me in the vehicle, and I thanked the nurse for her help. I briefly leaned my head back against the car's head rest and closed my eyes. Roy patted my leg, and we drove home.

My head was encircled in wide, thick bandages with an enormous amount over my right ear. I gingerly touched the thick padding with the tips of my fingers.

"You could hide a banana inside the bandages over my ear and never find it." I glanced at Roy, and raised an eye-brow.

He chuckled. "Yes, and maybe a Popsicle or two."

"I'm not going to let this get me down. Roy, I've already prayed."

"I have too."

Our daughters were with Bernice and Jimmy. We arrived to a quiet home, and Roy held my arm as I walked from the car to the front door. I felt weak, and he steered me to the living room. He didn't have to coax me into taking a nap. I approached the couch, gladly laid down, and fell asleep.

I awoke later, and Roy's parents were there. I could hear them talking in the kitchen. I heard the hinges squeak on the screen door as Roy and his dad's voices boomed about checking out the new lawn mower in the garage.

Lil with daughter, Rhonda, after mastoid ear surgery in Nov.1956

"Go on. I'm not interested." His mother laughed, and the screen door slammed shut.

"Mrs. Sehlke? Could you come into the living room? I'd like to talk to you." I sat up and leaned against the armrest.

She bustled into the room. "I didn't realize you were awake."

I smiled. "Haven't been for long."

She sat on the edge of the couch at the opposite end, and folded her hands in her lap. "I'm sorry to hear about your condition."

"Thank you." I straightened my posture and took a deep breath. "I wanted to talk to you about the children. My doctor gave me one week to live, and if that is true, I'd like to know that you as the only Grandmother would take care of the girls. Hopefully, I will survive, but just in case…"

"No." She interrupted me.

Wide-eyed, I starred at her in disbelief.

"What?' I whispered.

"No. I have already raised my children. I love them, and I love yours, but I won't raise anymore." She sprang from the couch, held her head high, and briskly left the room.

She proceeded to yell to her husband that she was ready to go. I'm certain my neighbors heard her request.

Roy and his dad came in from the garage, and his parents took off in a hurry. Roy ambled into the living room and sat beside me.

"How are you feeling?"

"Not near as weak, I need to eat something and try to get all of my strength back."

"Bernice brought a large dish of chicken and rice while you were asleep."

"She did?"

"Yes, and it smelt yummy." He pulled me up from the couch. "Let's try it."

I followed him into the kitchen, and he set the table. I took a pain pill while he heated the meal.

He said the blessing and filled our bowls.

I took the first bite. "Umm, good flavor, this is so sweet of Bernice." I paused. "How are the girls?"

"They are fine."

We continued eating. I waited until his bowl was almost empty. I had to discuss the conversation I had with his mother. It played over and over in my mind like a 45 RPM record with a skip on it.

"What's wrong? You're stirring your rice round and round."

I released the tight grip I had on the handle of my spoon, and fell silent. Frowning, I made eye contact with my husband, and took a deep breath.

"I ...uh...talked to your mother while ago, and asked her to look after the girls if I don't make it..."

Roy stiffened.

We continued eye contact.

"She said no. She said she already raised her kids and won't raise anymore."

He flicked his napkin across the table.

"Lil, you have to overlook her. She is old."

"She is a healthy, fifty-five year old who spoke to me completely devoid of emotion about her grandchildren."

"That's not fair."

"I am not going to argue with you about your mother. I am just shocked at what she said."

"Lil, she is not a young woman who can take care of kids."

"You are making excuses. You didn't hear her tone of voice."

"And you are making too much out of that conversation. Lil, your health and emotions are playing into your reaction of what she said."

"My reaction? Forget it, Roy. Let's stop this."

We put it behind us, and I grew stronger each day. I prayed and prayed and prayed. I lived another week, and another; thanking God constantly. My doctor was amazed at my progress. After my six week checkup, I gave thanks again to God, and still give Him all the glory.

Roy and I had our annual garden, and he taught Jayne how to water it using the long, water hose. She loved the responsibility. I couldn't get any water in my ear so it was strictly a Father and Daughter time together. Rhonda was too young to join them.

He brought home an additional water hose one evening, and he and Jayne ran outside to add it to the existing water hose. It now reached the entire length of the garden, and they were both excited. I watched from the kitchen window. Roy, full of mischief, suddenly sprayed Jayne with a stream of water, and she squealed. I knocked on the window, and he turned to grin at me when he dropped the hose. Jayne ran and grabbed it, pointing it at her dad. She laughingly drenched him. He was happy but wet. They both ran dripping wet around the back yard with the water hose.

Each time he'd try to walk closer to her to retrieve the hose, she would soak him. They had a lot of fun that day.

By this time, we sold our small house and searched for a larger home to buy in the same neighborhood. Several were about to be on the market. Meanwhile, we rented the parsonage across the street from the Lutheran Church we attended.

We had just moved, and the following week Roy's dad hurt his back again. He could no longer work. He and Roy's mother moved in with us due to financial problems. They had separate quarters with their own bathroom, but shared the kitchen we used. They had their own refrigerator, but wouldn't let their granddaughters open it.

    I remarked to Roy how I thought that was unusual.

    He made excuses.

    They checked for fingerprint smudges on the door of their refrigerator, and Roy made excuses again.

They would not let the granddaughters watch television in their room. They stayed in their room day and night, only coming out to talk to Roy. The three would laugh and enjoy lengthy conversations. They never talked to me or the girls.

It grew steadily worse, and Roy continued making excuses for his parents; they were old, they wanted privacy, etc. Some of it I could understand, but the arrangement wasn't working like we had planned. The girls would cry to see them and were ignored. Finally, I had enough. The daily stress wasn't worth it. I decided Roy and his parents could all have each other. I phoned my dad, and the girls and I left with him.

Lil's father, Robert Fritsche

We stayed at my daddy's house until I found a job and an apartment. I was happy raising my daughters as a single parent.

Chapter Nineteen

The Pastor asked Daddy for my new address, and Daddy gave it to him. Several Deacons from the Lutheran Church, and the Pastor, often came as a group to talk to me. They wanted me to reconcile with Roy and keep our family together.

Eventually, I gave in to their reasoning. Roy's parent's moved to Clute, Texas, and Roy and I bought a new, three bedroom home in a new subdivision in Houston. We were happy for a few years.

Roy had a lot of friends. He was well liked by everyone who knew him.

On week-ends, he invited friends over for cook-outs. Many were members of the Houston Police Department. We would enjoy fish-fry's, barbecue, or seafood. The social gatherings took their toll upon our family life and created a strain on our finances.

Although Roy worked full time at the same auto parts job he'd had for years, and received promotions, it became necessary for me to work, also. I got a full-time job at the

American Can Company working all night. I caught the city bus on the corner near our home to travel to work, and would arrive there in thirty minutes.

For safety reasons, I could not drive. I could barely hear the blast from the whistle of an approaching train. My hearing loss completely prevented me from obtaining a driver's license. I didn't mind at all. I enjoyed the bus ride; it was a relaxing time for me.

The arrangement worked well. My daughter Jayne was in school while I slept,

Rhonda would be across the street at the babysitters, and Roy would be at work. After I slept for several hours, I would cook meals for my family, clean the house, and wash clothes. I managed to keep up the pace by not tackling too many household chores in the same day.

Jayne was 10 years old and in the fifth grade the year I began working nights and Rhonda was five years old.

Lil with daughter's Jayne & Rhonda

I remember one particular morning, getting off the bus extremely weary, and walking one block home through our neighborhood. It was a Saturday morning, and I wouldn't have to wake Jayne for school or Rhonda for the babysitter. Roy worked Monday through Saturday, and I looked forward to going straight to sleep.

As I plodded home that day, I noticed a lot of furniture randomly sitting across my front yard. I gasped as I recognized every piece of furniture from my living room…

couch, chairs, end tables, lamps, coffee table, bookcase, etc. Staring in amazement, I stumbled and had to catch my balance.

I hurried. The closer I came the more I realized nothing was placed on the concrete driveway. The furniture was standing in soggy St. Augustine grass—freshly cut from the day before. Water was pouring out the open, front door of the living room. I spotted the water hose lying on the sidewalk, and it was also lying in the doorway going inside the house.

Frowning, I entered my home.

Jayne turned around and grinned at me.

"Mama, I'm helping you clean."

I gazed at the water gushing out from the hose she held, soaking my waxed hard-wood floors. My heart fell, but I couldn't break hers.

"Oh, Jayne." Sleep deprived, I struggled to say the right words without hurting her feelings.

"Is this enough water?"

"Yes, yes." I blinked, and ran outside to the water faucet. Trembling, I turned the handle as fast as possible and stopped the flow into my house.

Jayne was dragging the hose out when I returned. I stepped lightly into the house and retrieved the broom and mop.

"Honey, this was a sweet idea to help, but this is not how I clean. Next time please wait until I am home, and we can clean together, okay?"

"Okay."

I removed most of the water by sweeping it out the door. I handed Jayne the mop, and she pushed it across the floor in every direction. Thankfully, Rhonda was still asleep. I retrieved towels from the bathroom, and dried off furniture legs as I brought them back inside. Finally, I opened the windows, turned the attic fan on, and finished mopping spots that Jayne had missed.

"I made a mess, didn't I?" Her shoulders slumped.

"Yes, but that is alright. You know not to do that again." I smiled at her, and she straighten her thin frame to the tall girl she was.

"I'm going to sleep for a while. Don't go outside, and don't wake your sister. Umm, would you help me with something?"

Her face suddenly beamed. "Yes."

I handed her a towel. "You might find cut blades of grass stuck to the furniture. Try and get the grass off. Then you can play in your room."

"Okay, Mama."

I gave her a hug and kissed the top of her head. "That's my big girl." Shaking my head, I was still shocked that Jayne had managed to drag the living room furniture outside by herself. That was Jayne, though, always wanting to help me, and little Rhonda had the same sweet traits.

Hours later, I awoke hearing both of my daughters laughing and playing. I was still exhausted and knew they needed lunch. I phoned the neighbor lady across the street to babysit them while I went back to bed. She babysat each day I worked, and loved the girls. After walking the girls to her house, I slept for six more hours that day.

The get-togethers continued. Roy and I even played dominoes with the next door neighbors; Louis and his wife Billie. Louis was a large, burly guy, and Billie was a petite woman. They were a sweet couple and didn't have children. They often gave new dolls to Jayne and Rhonda. The girls would play dolls for hours. Roy would barbecue, and we'd invite them over to eat with us, later playing board games or dominoes.

I wanted a photo album of the girls and saved money for weeks to purchase a camera. The girls watched as I became familiar with using it, and were excited about the pictures. The first time I took Rhonda's picture she surprised me.

"Rhonda, be still. I'm going to take your picture."

She looked at me and shook her head.

"Wait." She said, and hurried to turn her back to me.

I immediately took a picture of her back. She whirled around to face me and smoothed her hair.

"I'm ready now." She smiled sweetly, and I hurried to get the picture.

Jayne enjoyed getting her picture taken also, and loved to pose. Purchasing the camera proved to be one of my best ideas. So many happy moments were saved in those pictures.

Roy started staying out late with his buddies once or twice a week. At first I didn't mind, but it became annoying. I mentioned this was not a family life style for the girls. He made one excuse after another about his friends. One friend had moved out of state and recently returned, someone else was an old Army buddy Roy hadn't seen in years, or a buddy invited him out on a fishing trip. It was constant. Eventually, his buddies followed him home from work, and played dominoes at our kitchen table. Cook-outs continued, and I wasn't happy about the many people coming and going from our home.

One night, Roy returned home late and pulled into Louis and Billie's driveway. It was an honest mistake. Most of the houses resembled each other except for the color of the trim around the eaves and windows. Each house had a concrete driveway, concrete sidewalk, concrete patio, and one small tree in the front yard.

At 11:15 pm my phone rang. It was Billie. I was getting ready for work, and she sounded groggy with sleep.

"Lil? Roy parked in our drive-way. He must think he is at home. Louis said he is trying to unlock our front door, and he can't get it to open."

"I am so sorry, Billie. Holler at him, and tell him he's at the wrong house."

"Louis didn't want to embarrass him."

"Just ask Louis to tell him. Roy has to come home before I can go to work."

"Alright, Lil."

"Thanks, Billie." I hung the receiver in the cradle on top of the telephone, and shook my head.

I was the one embarrassed. Fuming, I hurried through the house and peeped out the front window. Roy was backing out of Louis and Billie's driveway. His car lights flooded our living room as he pulled into our driveway.

Roy unlocked our door and immediately saw me standing in the middle of the room. He stepped inside and chuckled. "Can you believe what just happened?"

"Billie phoned me. I don't think it's funny."

"Lil..."

"I'm done, Roy. I can't live like this anymore." I grabbed my purse and walked outside to catch the bus.

This time I didn't let anyone convince me to stay married to Roy. If they wanted to try living with him, they could. I'd had enough.

Chapter Twenty

I quit working my night job, and once again, the girls and I moved in with my sweet, old Daddy. When the divorce was final, I found a day job and saved for an apartment. I found one in the Heights, and liked that section of town. So did the girls.

This was in the mid-1950's; Jayne was now in the seventh grade, and Rhonda was in the second grade. Jayne preferred to be called by her middle name, Lynn. I let Lynn ride the city bus as long as she asked for my permission, and as long as I knew exactly where she would be going. She constantly took her little sister everywhere she went.

A favorite stop for them was Retigg's Ice Cream Parlor at the SW corner of 14th Street and Yale in the Heights. Lynn took Rhonda to the Heights Library each week, also. It was a three story building with a narrow stairway snug inside against the wall. It would wind round and round as you climbed higher on it and was difficult to pass someone on it, or meet someone going down while you went up.

Carpeted, it was as quiet of a walk as one could ever imagine. The girls would find a cubbyhole area on the third floor, and stretch out by the wall to read the books they had chosen. It was a wonderful experience. They each brought home a different selection of books every week.

Roses were in bloom, and the scent was heavy in the air throughout the Heights. Lynn and Rhonda discovered a neighborhood with elaborate, wrought iron fences in each yard along the concrete sidewalks. On Courtlandt

Street, rose bushes spilled out through the fences. The girls would stroll along the sidewalks and often watch the elderly women watering their flowers in their own yards. With a flip of an arm, the ladies' heavy watering cans sprinkled the plants with a gentle spray of water. One such white-haired lady always smiled at them.

"You can pick some roses if you like. I have many, and you could take them home." She offered.

"Thank you, ma'am. We'll take some to Mother, and she will be surprised."

Carefully, a few were chosen and picked. These were carried on the bus and brought home to me. My daughters were kind, and trustworthy, yet knew to be leery of strangers.

I loved my job. I worked at Alfred Wire Cloth Company, and everyone was friendly. Once a month, employees would bring a casserole for lunch, and we'd share. I enjoyed tasting the various dishes. Once, my boss spotted me at the bus stop waiting for the next bus.

"He slowed his car and pulled over to the curb. "Do you need a ride?"

"No, thank you. I like the bus ride."

"Well, in that case, I'll see you tomorrow." He nodded and drove away.

After that encounter, we seemed to run into each other daily, literally. I'd be leaving the break room carrying an apple or an orange, and he'd be racing in holding an empty coffee cup. We collided twice, and laughed about it.

At the next monthly casserole lunch day, he ate some of my fried chicken, and I ate some of his homemade blackberry cobbler. We talked about our lives and grew more comfortable with each other. I informed him I was only interested in being friends, nothing more. He agreed, and I relaxed.

His name was Lloyd Shackelford, and he was older than I was. I liked the quietness about him, and he had a slow, mischievous smile. Lloyd was a Christian, a gentleman, and a tall, thin, attractive man. He cared about his employees and treated them with respect.

I told him I was divorced with one daughter in the second grade, and the other in the seventh grade.

This is when Lynn was taking the city bus across town to Frank M. Black Jr. High to finish the school team. It was the school she attended while we lived in our home with her father. She played the flute in band, and was a nurse's aide for her second period class. Many students roller skated every Friday night at a large rink, and Lynn wouldn't miss it. She loved roller skating. The music blared and bright lights shined down on the wooden floor as people of all ages skated around the rink.

I told Lloyd about it, and he suggested taking her to the Ice Palace. I did.

The Ice Palace had a round brick sitting area where you could sip your hot chocolate when taking a break from ice-skating. The skating rink was larger. Lynn rented her skates and fell a few times but thought it was neat. I had left Rhonda at the sitters. A people watcher, I enjoyed simply being there and didn't want to skate.

The following Monday, I thanked Lloyd for his suggestion of taking Lynn there.

Lloyd smiled and rubbed his chin. "Lil, I have another suggestion. I'd like to take you out to dinner next Friday evening while Lynn is skating, and Rhonda is at the sitters, if you want to go."

I was speechless, but I did want to go.

After being single for two years, I considered going on a date—my first since I was a teenager.

"Lloyd, I like your suggestion. Let's plan on the dinner."

"Yes, ma'am. Tell me your address, and what time to be there."

I jotted the address on a napkin along with my phone number, and the time to arrive. Handing it to him, I felt my heart race, and I hoped I wasn't blushing.

"See you later." I nodded and returned to my work area.

I turned, and looked back at him, and he winked at me.

That was the beginning of a big change in my life, and one for the better.

Chapter Twenty-One

Our dinner date was at a local restaurant I was not familiar with. After we'd eaten the delicious T-bone steak, baked potato, and salad we'd both ordered, Lloyd motioned for the waiter to refill our iced tea glasses. He was attentive and talkative throughout the meal. Completely relaxed, I listened to his stories, and realized Lloyd Shackelford was becoming more than a friend to me.

I also learned we had a lot in common, despite our fifteen year age difference. I was born in 1928, and raised in the country. He was born in 1913, and raised in Kellyville, a few miles out of Jefferson, Texas. His father had a lot of acreage and grew cotton. Lloyd had two brothers and four sisters. Country life was not new to him.

"There is a photo in the Jefferson Historical Society Museum showing my daddy driving a horse and wagon through downtown Jefferson. In the wagon, he hauled the first bale of cotton that season. Local residents filled the streets in celebration. If you look at the picture, you'd think you were seeing me. The difference is in what the people were wearing back in those days. I look exactly like my father."

"How did you end up in Houston?"

"We lived on the old homestead years after Daddy died. My brother, William, who was older than me, had married Ludie, a nurse. William is a night watchman at T.J. Blackburn Syrup Works in Jefferson. Ludie wanted their part of Daddy's property, so Mother was forced to sale. None of the other siblings wanted their part, but she had to sale it because of Ludie. William insisted he didn't want it. Anyway, Mother sold the property to H.G.Wells, and the home burnt in the following years." He took a sip of iced tea and quickly continued.

"My other brother, Dee Shackelford, moved to Sweetwater, Texas and my sisters; Mary, Maurine, and Jenny moved to Houston. My oldest sister, Ida, had died years earlier. Of course, William and Ludie remained in their home in Jefferson. I was one of the last to leave. I took Mother, and my son with me. We moved to Houston, and lived together until Wendell moved off to college."

"You have a son?"

"Yes, he's married now, and he has a son. I'm a grandfather."

"You're a grandfather." I blurted, wide-eyed.

He nodded as a half-smile suddenly appeared.

"And what happened to your wife, if you don't mind me asking?"

"She ran off with a truck driver one day. I had no idea she even knew him. Anyway, I came home from work and found the baby alone, sitting on the living room floor, crying. She was gone." He raised his eyebrows.

"Gone? And left the baby by himself?"

"Yes ma'am. She returned for her clothes a week later. Wendell was seven months old. I had placed him on a pallet with some toys. When she walked in, he started crying. I entered the living room from the kitchen, and saw her kick the baby. He rolled across the floor, and I rushed to him. I ordered her out of the house. I had never seen her hurt him before, and I vowed she never would again. I got a divorce and was granted full custody of my son. Mother helped take care of Wendell while I worked."

"How can anyone hurt a helpless baby?" I shook my head, frowning.

"I don't know. I thought I knew her." He paused. "So now you know why I never remarried…hard to trust, again." He smiled.

"I know. My marriage ended when my husband's social life came first. I've been divorced two years, and haven't dated, didn't even want to date."

"I'm glad you didn't, my dear. I believe God has a plan for everything and everyone."

"Yes, and when we do our will, instead of His will, nothing works out as you planned. And I know, as a couple not doing God's will, there are many problems made by someone's bad choices. You should know something else about me, I also believe in the power of prayer."

"So do I, and you should always put God and family first, in that order. If its Gods will, anything you do after that will easily fall in place. You won't encounter any obstacles."

We nodded, and I experienced an overwhelming peaceful feeling. Although content to remain at the table and talk for hours, I thought of my children and glanced at my watch.

"Don't worry. We'll make it in time." He smiled reassuringly, stood and placed a tip beside his plate. The waiter hurried, and gave him the ticket. Lloyd paid it, and we were inside his car in less than five minutes.

He drove me to each place to get the girls. They seemed to like Lloyd. He told them amusing stories as he maneuvered the car through late-night city traffic. Shortly after 10 pm, he dropped us off at my apartment. Before he left, plans were already made for our next date.

It became our routine to include the girls on every other date, and enjoy an event or family activity together. The girls liked playing miniature golf with us. We took them to the car races, to the beach in Galveston, and once we happened upon a country and western concert.

We were driving down Little York one Saturday and noticed a crowd in a shopping center's parking lot. The people surrounded a flatbed, eighteen-wheeler truck that had musicians and singers performing on the flatbed of the trucks' trailer.

Texas Ruby sang, followed by Red Foley, and a few others. Minnie Pearl yodeled, and later told a joke about the awful smell at Pasadena, Texas and called it Stink-A-Dena, Texas. It was exciting, and everyone yelled for more when the performance ended.

I don't know what we enjoyed more, that performance or little Rhonda walking around for days singing loudly and attempting to yodel. We had to turn our faces away from her, so she couldn't see our smiles. Sometimes a 'yoda- lady-who' yodel turned into a 'cocka-doodle–do' rooster crow.

"Okay, it's time to take your city girls to the country." Lloyd teased. "I've wanted to show you my hometown, anyway. Rolling hills and tall pine trees can't be beat."

"Concrete buildings haven't got a chance." I chimed in.

"Exactly."

We left the next Saturday, and stopped at an Indian Reservation in Livingston, Texas. Lloyd bought the girls souvenirs, and they talked non-stop as we drove north. We discovered another whole new world in Northeast Texas. Lloyd was right, the girls needed to be exposed to the country, and they loved it. He showed Lynn how to use the movie camera. She stretched out in the back of the station wagon and recorded the road behind us as we traveled up and down over the hills and valleys.

Fenced pastures, animals, crops growing, and trees fascinated the girls. Rhonda would ask Lynn about anything that was new to them, and Lynn, being the big girl who enjoyed explaining anything to Rhonda when given the opportunity…was not at a loss when she asked about cows.

They were sitting in the back seat at this time, Lloyd was driving, and I sat in the front seat beside him. We could easily overhear the girl's conversations.

"What kind of cow is that?" Rhonda pointed to one grazing in a pasture as we passed by on the highway.

"Oh, that's a bull. He is always the largest of all cows." Lynn informed her younger sister.

We drove on and came upon a barn with another fenced in area filled with cows.

"Well, what are those?"

"Those are milk cows."

Farther down the highway we approached another pasture of cows, and Rhonda again questioned Lynn.

"What kind are they?"

"Well, they are not bulls, and they are not milk cows, so they have to be just plain cow-cows." Lynn was serious, and Rhonda solemnly nodded.

I tried not to snicker, and Lloyd poked me in my ribs. We didn't set the cow story straight until a later time.

Lloyd gave us quite a tour. Jefferson is rich in history; Caddo Lake and Lake O' The Pines are both beautiful and unique in their own way. Caddo Lake has moss hanging from the branches of Cypress trees in and out of the water, and Lake O' The Pines has large expansions of water with swimming areas. Boating and fishing in either looked inviting.

We returned to Houston after our one day trip. We had left extremely early and arrived home late that night.

Someone told Roy about our trip. He came to visit the girls later, and tried to talk me into re-marrying him. I refused. He became angry then, and said I sure didn't need to marry Lloyd because he was an old man—way too old for me.

Another year of dating, and Lloyd and I married.

The girls and I met Lloyd's mother, Mirtie, before the wedding, and yes, it turned out she was the same elderly woman on

Courtlandt Street that Lynn and Rhonda had already met and picked her roses.

Myrtie's daughter, Maurine and her husband Harold lived a few houses up from her on the same side of the street.

The girls had walked past the houses of future family members and naturally had no idea, or that the sweet, elderly woman would one day be their step-grandmother.

Lil Shackelford, Mirtie Bell Shackelford (Lloyd's mother), & Lloyd Shackelford

We let Lynn transfer to Hamilton Jr. High after we married. Her new Aunt Maurine and Uncle Harold Terry worked there. Maurine was the school nurse, and Harold was a history teacher. Lynn enjoyed visiting them often after school. She also worked the school popcorn machine and made popcorn every Friday after lunch. She was thrilled to get the job, and did well at it.

Lloyd and I bought Rhonda a pair of cheerleader pom-poms, and a baton to twirl. She was delighted. We bought Lynn a camera, and a small tape recorder. She kept us all on alert for candid pictures she'd take of us when we weren't expecting it. Lynn loved to place the recorder under the dining room table and turn it on while we were eating and talking. Besides our talking, you could hear lots of knives and forks clinking together loudly. It seems we were a noisy bunch during dinner. She took some pictures at the dining room table and one caught our facial expressions perfectly as Rhonda got reprimanded. It was cute, but embarrassing.

In that picture, Rhonda, serious and bold, glanced at Lloyd's plate and then looked him straight in his face. "That is the fourth piece of fried chicken you have eaten," she announced. Lloyd pointed his finger at her and said, "I can eat however many I want." I frowned at him, and Lynn instantly appeared in the doorway with the camera and captured the moment. Lloyd was still pointing his finger at Rhonda, and she was pouting. Priceless. Rhonda never counted what he ate again.

We later moved to Jefferson, Texas.

Lynn began writing huge letters to our family in Houston describing life in the country. She also loved riding horses. Rhonda loved her new puppy. Me, I loved my husband and became his constant companion. We fished together, gardened together, canned vegetables together and worshiped in church together. There wasn't a Lutheran church in the area, so the girls and I attended my husband's Methodist church with him. It was similar to the faith I was raised on, and I was one happy woman.

I did miss my large family. One year, instead of having my family reunion in Houston, they came to visit us, and loved Northeast Texas as much as we did. It was a special time with fond memories for everyone.

One day Rhonda went out to play in the neighborhood. She had announced earlier that she was going to get a job. We became concerned hours later when she didn't return, after all, she was only seven years old. She came strolling through the yard as Lloyd and I were leaving in the car to search for her.

"Where have you been?" I hurried out of the vehicle and marched in her direction.

"I told you I was going to get a job." She put her hands on her hips.

"What did you do, young lady?"

"I walked to town, and asked the man at the five and dime store if I could have a job today, and he let me dust. I got the job." She grinned, and although I was actually proud of her, I had to tell her not to do that again.

That spring, Lloyd bought Lynn a 22 single shot Remington rifle. She became an expert shot at target practice. He taught her how to track animals, but she couldn't shoot one. She enjoyed identifying their tracks and quietly followed them. We sent her with her rifle to retrieve the mail from our rural mailbox. It was two miles down the dirt road from our home, and no, we didn't have any neighbors. Country living was busy and pleasant.

We had a large garden. The girls would sing there to the top of their lungs as we worked. Clods of dirt lying on top of the newly plowed rows had to have weeds removed. They'd pull them out, toss the weeds into a pile, and keep singing. The dog joined in and as they sang loudly, he tilted his head back and howled just as loud. It was a lot of fun.

That summer, we put Lynn on the train at the old depot in Jefferson, Texas. Roy was to meet her in Brenham, Texas. His mother, Martha Sehlke, had died. His dad, Oscar Julius Sehlke had died earlier. Oscar often had massive nose bleeds and was rushed by ambulance to the hospital. I don't remember how Oscar or Martha died, or when they moved back to Brenham from Clute, Texas; but Lynn was old enough to ride the train to Brenham. Rhonda was far too young to travel.

Roy's only sibling, his brother, Tex, was there from Minnesota. The two brothers were taking care of their parents' estate.

Roy met Lynn at the Brenham train station, and they drove to his parents' home. She met her Uncle Tex there as they walked from room to room in the house. It was full of furniture, and Lynn was amazed at one tall, elaborately carved, wooden cabinet with glass doors. It held Martha's collection of over fifty porcelain dolls in perfect condition each wearing billowing southern belle dresses.

It remains a mystery as to why Lynn and Rhonda didn't receive even one doll. Perhaps their grandparent's affairs required selling their possessions to pay for any debt they may have acquired.

Roy and his brother concluded their task and locked the doors on their parents' home. Tex left for Minnesota, and Roy drove Lynn back to his apartment in Houston. She stayed with him for a few weeks.

One day while he was at work, Lynn put a coconut in his porcelain kitchen sink. She hit it with a hammer, and the impact busted the sink into pieces. Roy was renting. He had to explain to his landlord what had happened, and that he would pay to have a new sink installed. He never became angry with Lynn, but advised her to open any future coconuts outside on a concrete surface.

Lloyd, the girls, and I moved from Jefferson, Texas to live on Caddo Lake in Karnack, Texas. A devout Methodist, Lloyd would occasionally preach as a layman. We all treasured hearing Lloyd's sermons.

Years went by, and Lynn married.

Lloyd had bought a brand new car, a yellow Javelin. I talked Lloyd into teaching Rhonda how to drive—she was old enough. He was happy to teach her.

With Rhonda at the wheel, and Lloyd sitting in the front passenger's seat, they approached a curve in the black-top country road.

"Don't go in the ditch, Rhonda, it's full of water."

She turned the steering wheel to maneuver around the curve, and drove the brand new car straight into the ditch. Lloyd didn't get mad, though. He had a lot of patience, and continued teaching her. Rhonda soon mastered the necessary skills and obtained her driving license.

Roy later died in a V.A. hospital. He had cancer of the stomach and liver. The hospital contacted Lynn about his death, and stated they wanted his personal possessions removed. The girls, both married by this time, drove with Lynn's two sons across the state to Temple, Texas to collect his belongings. His funeral had been pre-arranged, and they arrived in time to view the body. It was a sad trip for all.

During the last years of marriage to Lloyd, and enjoying our increased family with grandchildren, Lloyd became seriously ill. He died on August 9, 1987 on the exact day of our twenty-fifth wedding anniversary. He died of emphysema and lung disease. He had previous surgery removing parts of his lungs. They were black with tar and badly damaged.

Lloyd smoked unfiltered Pall Mall cigarettes. Before he died, he was wheezing horribly, yet managed to talk as our entire family surrounded him in his hospital bed that day. He wanted us to promise not to keep smoking if we did smoke, and never to start smoking if we didn't. He said it was just too painful. We promised.

Lloyd was the rock of our family, and deeply missed.

It was seven years later, but felt like ten years, that I remarried. Lynn introduced me to R. D. Clark. He was a friend of a deputy Lynn knew. He had been divorced for fourteen years, and also had a daughter named Rhonda. He was one great guy.

We married on February 7, 1994, and we thought his health was excellent. We bought a mobile home and moved to Scottsville, Texas. He was later rushed to the hospital from our home, and died due to hemorrhaging of the brain on December 27, 1994.

I never dated or remarried again. However, my old school friend, Mary Ellen, and I continued to keep in touch with each other throughout the years. She re-married years after her husband died. Mary Ellen re-married at the age of 83, and lives in South Louisiana.

R.D. & Lil Clark were married on Feb 7,1994. R.D passed away on Dec 27,1994

PART III

Chapter Twenty-Two

The year is 2015, and I am blessed with another birthday. I have reached the age of 87 years old. I strongly believe in the power of prayer, and I am now a member of Karnack Baptist Church in Karnack, Texas. If you aren't attending a church, please try mine. Our pastor preaches straight from the Bible, it's always a learning experience.

My younger sister, Bernice, passed away about seven years ago. Raymond, my younger brother, died in 1970. I raised both of them and know they believed in Jesus Christ. He is our Savior. They are in Heaven now, and I am comforted, but I do miss them both every day.

If you want Jesus for your Savior, please pray:

Dear God in heaven, I come to You in the name of Jesus. I am a sinner, and I am sorry for my sins, and the life I have lived; I pray for forgiveness. I believe Your only begotten Son Jesus Christ shed His precious blood on the cross at Calvary and died for my sins, and I am now willing to turn from my sin.

You said in Your Holy Word, Romans 10: 9 that if we confess to the Lord our God and believe in our hearts that God raised Jesus from the dead, we shall be saved. Right now I confess Jesus as the Lord of my soul. With my heart, I believe that God raised Jesus from the dead. This very moment I accept Jesus Christ as my own personal Savior and according to His Word, right now I am saved.

Thank You, Jesus, for Your unlimited grace which has saved me from my sins. I thank You, Jesus, that Your grace always leads to repentance. I pray, Lord Jesus, transform my life so that I may bring glory and honor to You alone and not to myself. Thank You, Jesus, for dying for me and giving me eternal life. Amen.

Bernice was in a nursing home in south Texas. She had heart trouble and loved the home she resided in until I would phone. Then she wanted to come and stay with me, and I'd have to remind her she needed to be close to her doctors as I live a five hour drive away from them. Besides, I couldn't drive, but she had forgotten that. I phoned her at least once a week and would mail her packages of items she wanted. Once, she told me it was too cold there, and she needed a sweater. I mailed one to her with many books to read, also. She and I loved to read, and we had swapped books with each other for over forty years.

One day I dialed her number and there was no answer. It rang and rang. I kept calling. A nurse finally answered the phone after I let it ring for a few minutes. I told her I was Bernice's sister and wanted to talk to her.

Silence.

"Ma'am? Are you there?"

"Yes." She paused. "No one has told you?"

"Told me what?" I demanded.

"I'm so sorry. Your sister passed away this morning. I was with her. We were talking and she was laughing…so happy… and suddenly, she slumped over dead with a massive heart attack. I'm so sorry to have to tell you like this."

I was stunned and couldn't speak. Crying, I thanked her for telling me and quickly hung up the phone.

Raymond had been happy too before he died. He went elk hunting in Colorado with our brothers; Otto, Ernest, Rubin, and Rudolph. His life ended so tragically, though. Raymond was gut shot while on a ledge. The weapon used was from someone not registered to be on the hunting lease and could not be traced. No charges could be filed. My other brothers never went hunting again.

I only have three living family members. My sister Lorraine was born in 1925, is now 90 years old, and lives alone in Iowa. We phone each other often, and I send her large print books to read.

My sister Elsie was born in 1920, is now 95 years old, and lives in Spring, Texas with her daughter who is going blind and whose husband has cancer. Their daughter comes to take care of them. Elsie has heart problems and some memory loss. No one will let her use the phone. We were told she was agreeing to buy whatever product any telemarketer tried to sell her. Elsie's doctor didn't want her stressed, so suggested she be kept off the phone. Her grandchildren had nicknamed her, 'Grambo' when the Rambo movies were popular. It fit her well. She was small, but not afraid to speak up if someone did something wrong. I'm sure they all try to keep her from stressing on different issues.

We haven't been allowed to talk to Elsie in years. The last time I talked to Elsie she told me she didn't have any money. She said the government quit sending her social security check to her. I told her they don't simply stop sending it, and she was shocked. After that, Elsie's daughter wouldn't let her talk to any of us sisters. I realize now, that was how they justified her not buying anything over the telephone; they simply told her she didn't have any money.

My sister Marie was born in 1919, is now 96 years old, and lives in Lufkin, Texas with her daughter. We phone each other and share recipes. A few years ago, she spent about four months with me. We set my sewing machine up on a large table and made Pouting Dolls. Each one had to be stuffed and sewn, so we organized an assembly line. It was a lot of fun to shop for material to make their clothes, and buy their little hats and shoes. We made and sold hundreds of them. They have their arms crossed in front of their heads with their faces hidden. They were two feet tall and adorable with their matching accessories.

When you walk into Lynn's house, she has two of the Pouting Dolls in her foyer standing against the wall with their back to you, pouting. One is a girl wearing a straw hat with a long pink ribbon that hangs over the back of her pink and white dress. The dress has pastel flowers on the material, overlaid with white lace, and the same type of pink ribbon sewn into a section of the lace. She has on pink Mary Jane shoes, and has a pink straw basket of wildflowers. Next to her is the boy. He is wearing a blue denim floppy hat, and has on "My Kid" bluejeans with a red, white and blue hoodie printed in teddy bears with the hood part in solid red hanging down his back. He has on red, white and blue "My Kid" tennis shoes, and a slingshot hanging out of his back pocket. They are both so cute!

Lorraine, Marie and I still enjoy cooking. We don't know what Elsie does or does not do. We were told she was happy, but she must wonder why she doesn't hear from her sisters.

A few years ago we had a sister letter. One of us would start it, and mail it to the next sister. That one would insert a letter with news about herself, and her family, and send all of it to the next sister, on and on it went. We couldn't wait to receive it in the mail. It was a lot of fun. Now, since we are so few in numbers, and our handwriting is becoming shaky, it is easier to phone.

I had been living in Scottsville, Texas when my husband, R D, passed away. I was alone and didn't drive. Lynn didn't want me living thirty miles away from her and wanted me to move by her. She also had a long drive to take me to my doctors' appointments, etc. when I needed to go. I decided to move my mobile home onto her property, and she became my caregiver. I live next door to her now, and we are best friends. Lynn also takes me to grocery stores, church, the post office, movie theaters, restaurants, book signings, etc. She is a published Christian author and is writing her next Christian Fiction series. I am very proud of her. Besides helping me daily, she keeps a watchful eye on my home, her house, and her two rent houses. A few weeks ago, someone started pounding on the side of my home at three o'clock in the morning and running away. Lynn had flood lights installed all over the area. The mischief stopped immediately. Now, we resemble a small town at night with enough light to illuminate a football field at a championship game.

She lives alone, and we make a great team. We can handle all that life gives us to handle and sometimes that's a lot. But with God's help, we pull through it, and I'm so glad she insisted I move by her. I love it. She has two sons, three grandchildren, and two great grandchildren.

We can enjoy our morning coffee on her back deck watching the river roll by and hear the birds chirping. It is so peaceful and relaxing. We take turns cooking, enjoy playing card games when stormy weather keeps us indoors, and we both sew and can vegetables. Of course, she writes every day, and I read a lot.

Rhonda lives in Louisiana. She has one daughter, one son, two grandchildren, and two great grandchildren. I am blessed by all of my grandchildren. Out of the four grandchildren I have from Lynn and Rhonda, I have one great, grandchild, Dustin, who was born on my birthday. He has a new born son, and an older son; my two great, great-grandchildren. Rhonda always has a birthday party for me and her grandson, Dustin, together. When his son, Bradley, was four years old, I attended his birthday party. Bradley had been told earlier that I am his great, great grandmother. They live out of state so I don't get to visit with them often, but Bradley recognized me, and was glad to see me. As he reached to open my present to him, his mother told him it was from me and pointed towards me. He was thrilled. As he ripped the wrappings off the package, his face beamed, and he exclaimed, "This is from my Great-great-great-great-great Grandma." We laughed at the many 'greats' he added. How sweet he remembered me.

Rhonda is an interior decorator, and she's amazing at it. I'm very proud of her, also. She decorates homes; new and old, banks, businesses, etc. She decorates for most holidays and does graduations, and birthdays. She has many new and repeat customers, and they keep her busy! She has made numerous items using wood and is just as comfortable with a skill saw as she is creating a wreath or a flower arrangement. When I visit her, we go shopping, and she always wants me to stay longer. I love her, and love being with her, but I miss my home and want to return to it. The older I get, the more I want to stay home. I guess we really are creatures of habit and enjoy our own routine.

Through the years I'm been fortunate with my health. I've had three, total hip-replacements, one hip re-done twice, and the other one is still functional. I bought new hearing aids last year and for the first time, I could hear out of both ears. My old eye, ear, nose and throat specialist never did a CT scan, and treated me for a drainage problem in my left ear for over eight years. He would use a suction instrument to clean it out and go deep into my ear. It hurt me so badly that I quit going to him. In the records he sent to my new doctor, he stated I had chronic drainage as it has drained off and on for years. It would clog the microphone tip of the hearing aid. My new eye, ear, nose, and throat specialist did a CT scan and said my eardrum was deteriorating and causing the drainage. I'd only had four appointments with him, and he said he couldn't do anything else for me as I am allergic to many drops that could help. I didn't want surgery at my age but did agree to my ear doctor referring me and making an appointment for me in Dallas, Texas at the Ear Institute.

After the specialist in Dallas examined my ears, and the CT scan, I gave thanks to God again. I now have a doctor that diagnosed the problem and is skilled at correcting it. He said I had a collapsed eardrum in my left ear but the worse problem was a cyst behind the eardrum. It had attached to and was eating away at the bone of my skull.

All of those eight years that my first 'specialist' had treated me, he never did any tests. The second 'specialist' did a CT scan, but couldn't read it correctly. I never had a chance with those two doctors, but thank God the second doctor made the appointment with the specialist in Dallas! My new doctor in Dallas had to remove the cyst. He said I was a walking time bomb, and my condition would worsen to the point that I could be paralyzed, etc. It would take him two hours to operate, and it would be day surgery.

We all prayed about it and felt like God provided this doctor who is in the routine of doing this type of surgery. Of course, risks and complications are always considered. I had the surgery, a tympanoplasty/mastoidectom, on July 22, 2015. Drainage has stopped, no fever, and I am no longer on pain pills. Dizziness is gone. I am back to cooking and enjoyed a sewing project last week. I still haven't completely healed inside my ear, and can't hear anything. This was expected, though. People write notes to me instead of talking, and I read closed captioning on television. I should be able to wear my hearing aids by the end of October. Thank God the worst is over! I am so blessed with such a caring family, friends, and church family. They have helped me through a lot with this surgery, and I give thanks for all of them daily.

I had a few falls and have to be careful where I step. I now have a life-alert button on a chain I wear around my neck. I haven't had to push the button for help. The fact that I am wearing it reminds me to walk slower and be more cautious.

I have pot plants, hanging baskets, a rose garden overflowing with mint, and grow vegetables in flower pots now. I enjoy the birds and squirrels, and have several bird feeders hanging from my dogwood tree. I love being outside, cleaning out my flower beds, pulling weeds, and clipping the tops of my Gardenia and Azalea bushes when they need trimming.

Lynn can glance out her window and see me outside working on some project. She calls me the energizer bunny from the television commercials. She said it looks like someone wound me up, and I keep going all over the lawn.

After a few hours, she'll suggest I need to rest. I do have a tendency to try and complete too much in one day. When I see

Lynn bringing me a cold bottle of water, I know it's time to stop. I have to give Lynn credit, she is a great caregiver.

I enjoy relaxing in my recliner by either reading or working a word-search puzzle. My favorite treat while I rest is the delicious homemade fudge made by Brandon and Billie Bradbury. I love the raspberry-pecan-cheesecake fudge, rocky road fudge, chocolate amaretto swirl, and chocolate mint swirl, plain fudge, cinnamon roll fudge…I could go on and on, there is such a variety. I do love their fudge. Yum!

If you are ever in downtown Marshall, Texas; drive by 208 N. Washington and stop in at Blissmoor Valley Ranch Company Store. They are wonderful people and even let you sample the fudge. ☺

God is good all the time, and all the time God is good!

The End

Acknowledgments

I give God the glory, and honor, and praise for His guidance that went into this work.

I would like to thank the following people for their help with the book;

Jeff Brannon, my son, for working the manuscript into his busy schedule and not only editing it, but publishing it as well,

Lillie Clark, my mother, and her sisters, Marie Proske and Lorraine Hanson, for being so patient when I'd ask more questions gathering facts, documents, and in-depth details of what actually happened many years ago, and Bob and Amy Bell for an honest critique of the manuscript.

Family Photos

Lil, sister Bernice, brother Raymond with his son Darryl.

Lil and some of her siblings. Left to right. Otto, Ernst, Rubin, Bill, Olga, Bernice, Tilda, Lil, Raymond, Marie, & Elsie.

Lil's parents; Robert and Martha with Lil's siblings including herself on Robert & Martha's 25 Wedding Anniversary.

Back row: Tilda, Ed, Olga, Otto, Ernst, Amanda, Jane, Marie, Elsie
Front rows: Lil, Robert holding Bernice, Lorraine, Martha holding Raymond, Rubin and Bill.

The photographer put a silver flower in Robert's lapel, and a silver wreath of flowers around Martha's head. Everything on the table was their family silver. The picture cost them $25.00. Martha died a few years after this picture of their 25th Silver anniversary and also this picture includes their 15 children. (#16 was Freddie, and he died as a baby.)

Robert Fritsche's siblings and his parents. Ernst and Maria Schramm Fritsche.

Back row : Left to right ; Walter, Robert, Dora, Willie, Ester, Louis, Rosie, and Martin.

The Dannahaus family. (Roy Sehlke's grandparents and aunts and uncles except for the smallest girl. Martha Dannhaus is the smallest girl, and also the future Mother of Roy Sehlke.

Lil's mother, Martha's, parents. Mr. & Mrs. Mitschke.

Lil Fritsche, 16 years old.

Lil's Recipes

Candied Carrots

2 lbs. Carrots
2 Tbsp. Butter
½ cup Mrs. Butterworths syrup
Boiling water

Peel carrots, cut diagonally into one inch slices. Put in 2 qt. Saucepan, add boiling water to cover carrots by one inch, and simmer twenty minutes until tender. Drain. Add butter and toss well. Add syrup, heat and roll carrots in syrup until evenly glazed. Cook over medium heat until well glazed. Watch carefully to prevent scorching.

Salmon Patties

1 can salmon with juice
1 chopped onion, large
2 raw eggs
½ cup crumbled crackers

Mix well and shape into patties. Press each patty into corn meal, covering both sides.

Fry in hot oil turning several times until thoroughly cooked and golden brown.

Dressing

1 pan of cornbread
4 slices dark toast
2 cups finely chopped onion
1 ½ cups chopped celery
½ cup thinly sliced green onion
2 or 3 Tbsp. sage
Salt and pepper to taste
5 raw eggs
(3 or more cans of chicken broth, enough to be slightly soupy; unless you add boiled chicken.)

I cut up some boiled chicken and put it into the dressing, and use that broth; if it isn't enough to make it soupy, add broth from a can or two.

Mix well. Place it in a large, oiled pan. Cover with foil. Bake at 400 degrees for 45 minutes or until light brown on top.

Cucumber and Onion Salad

4 or 5 large cucumbers, sliced thin
1 large onion, sliced thin
¾ cup apple cider vinegar mixed with ¾ cup water
¼ teaspoon pepper
¾ teaspoon salt

Place cucumbers in a bowl. Sprinkle salt over them and let sit for about an hour. (The salt draws liquid out of the cucumbers.) Squeeze the liquid out and add the sliced onions. Mix with vinegar/water mixture and pepper. Place in fridge to cool.

This is a delicious German recipe.

Chicken Biscuit Bake

1 ¼ cup chopped onion
3 tbsp. butter
3 tbsp. flour
½ tsp. salt
1 ½ cups chicken broth
2 cups cooked, cubed chicken
1 cup cooked or canned peas
1 3oz. jar sliced mushrooms
1 cup cooked sliced carrots
2 tbsp. chopped pimento
1 pan of biscuits uncooked

Cook onion in butter until tender. Blend in flour and salt. Add broth all at once; cook and stir until thickened and bubbly. Add chicken and vegetables and heat until bubbly. Pour into 1 ½ qt. casserole dish. Cut each biscuit into 4 quarters. Arrange biscuits on top of casserole and bake at 425 degrees for 8-10 minutes or until biscuits are done.

Other books available by

Author Lynn Hobbs:

The Running Forward Series, a powerful faith and family saga:

Book One: Sin, Secrets, and Salvation… Awarded 1st place, 2013, in Religious Fiction by the Texas Association of Authors

Book Two: River Town…Awarded 1st Place, 2014, in Religious Fiction by the Texas Association of Authors

Book Three: Hidden Creek…Awarded 1st place, 2015, by the Texas Association of Authors

My goal in writing the series was to show readers a Christian viewpoint by the actions of my main fictional character, Susan Penleigh, as she experienced modern day problems.

My goal in writing the inspiring, true story of the life of my mother, 'Lillie, a Motherless Child', was to share moments that will not be lost in time, and to display her faith and determination in what she encountered.

All books are available on Amazon.com in either paperback or e-book format. Reader reviews on Amazon, Goodreads, and Kindle are always appreciated. I enjoy hearing from my readers; check out my website and contact me there at http://LynnHobbsAuthor.com

A word from the publisher:

LIKE THE BOOK?
HELP THE AUTHOR!
REVIEWS HELP WITH FUTURE SALES
GIVE A REVIEW ON AMAZON.COM

Did you know? Authors are not rich. In fact, most make less than $10,000. a year. Being an author is small business.

If there are 50 reviews, Amazon lists a book in its newsletters and other promotions. (Also "boughts".)

REVIEWS are the easiest way to say THANK YOU to the author and tell their publisher to produce more books

SUPPORT AUTHORS

SUPPORT SMALL BUSINESS

What to do!

1. Go to Amazon.com
2. In the long, blank search window at top of page, left hand corner; type in book title.
3. Click on the book title.
4. Click on the hyperlink that says… customer reviews.
5. Then click on the hyperlink that says…write a customer review.
6. Click on the number of stars you want to give (5 are best).

7. Type in the comment area to write your review: they can be short, for example…"I like it." It's the number of reviews that matters most.

A good review is like gold to an author. If you have ever bought anything on amazon, you automatically have an account, and can write a review.

Reviews are sincerely appreciated.

Thank you!

On the next few pages, check out some more great books from the publisher!

Need help getting published? Visit us today at ProofProductions.us

The Nephilim, A Giant Walk Through History
By: Jeff E. Brannon

A Biblically based, mostly historic, fictional story starting from the time of Jared (Noah's grand-father) through the present day. The word Nephilim is translated in Gen 6:1 as giant, but means "from the fallen ones". They were the offspring from the Fallen Angels and the daughters of Adam. It is an exciting adventure filled with historical content designed to be a springboard for the reader to explore a side of history often not told. I believe one cannot fully comprehend the Old Testament without understanding the role the Nephilim played. This book helps answer questions like, "If God is a God of love, why did He allow genocide in the OT?" and "What did Jesus mean that the last days would be like the days of Noah?" The book pulls from Ancient Biblical text as well as scrolls found along the Dead Sea Scrolls such as The Book of Giants. The synchronized, Biblically endorsed, extra-Biblical texts such as 1 Enoch, Jasher, and Jubilees also contribute to the historical accuracy of the narrative. Find out about the Vimana mentioned in over 1,000 text in ancient writings and how they tie in with the Nephilim and Watcher-class angels. This book answers questions the modern church typically runs from in an exciting story-driven narrative that puts the reader right in the middle of the action. In this story, the author takes you on a journey from the dawn of time through the present day and even portrays a glimpse in what might happen in the very near future. Who were Nimrod and his wife? How do they tie in to events both in the past and the future? Who are the Nephilim? Are they real? Do they live among us? Find out the answers to these and many more questions in this book today.

CHILDREN OF IRIS: REBORN
By: Raven Quill & Draeden Quill

"Something extraordinary has happened. Due to a happy accident with our logistics division we have been handed an opportunity to push the boundaries on a global stage." Leon replied without looking from the screen. "So we are training them to be soldiers?" "No, no. We don't need more soldiers. We need something better. We have a chance to eliminate the need for war all together. When you control the monster, what is there left to fear?" On a fateful fall day in Texas, Luke Jones is stabbed, burned, and left for dead while, in a nearby city, Francis Guy is mugged, bludgeoned and left to the same fate. They awaken, not only alive and fully healed, but captured by an indomitable government agency. There, Jones and Guy discover they have been gifted with super-human like abilities as they are forced to undergo one life threatening trial after another. With only each other for support, Jones and Guy become a formidable team as they are pitted against others with abilities beyond imagination. When faced with a grim ultimatum, they perform a daring escape back into the free world, leaving smoke and bodies in their wake. With nowhere to run and their very lives at stake, the duo split up in an attempt to take down this ruthless organization with the very same powers they were being trained to use. Thrown into a series of extraordinary circumstances, they meet both friend and foe alike as the battles they waged in captivity prove more and more useful. Will they drown under a sea of government conspiracy or will they rise from the ashes of their former lives and be reborn?

Eyes of a Neighbor

by Lynn Hobbs

"Eyes of a Neighbor" is book one of Lynn Hobbs new Christian Fiction series. The American Neighborhood Series will consist of three books. The reader can expect to find real life situations that will be surprising. Her stories don't have profanity or violence, but neither do they follow "cookie-cutter" plots. Boy may meet girl and marry girl, but typical, romantic, happy endings are not always guaranteed. In Eyes of a Neighbor, you are introduced to a community with its residents of newcomers, and those who have lived most of their lives in this older, historical section of Houston, Texas. Based on the author's own knowledge of having once lived in the Heights area, the residents she created include all age groups, and become tangled in a murder mystery. Suspense, intrigue, inspiration, and romance intertwine to create a fast paced read that is indeed a page turner.

Available in large print, the story continues in book two, Heart of a Neighbor; to be released in 2017. A third book will complete the series.

www.ingramcontent.com/pod-product-compliance
Lightning Source LLC
Chambersburg PA
CBHW070547100426
42744CB00006B/243